the power of breath
and hand yoga

the power of breath and hand yoga

pranayama and mudras for health and well-being

christine burke

CICO BOOKS

LONDON NEW YORK

This book is dedicated to Clementine, who always holds my hand, and to all of the precious hands who hold this book.

Published in 2019 by CICO Books
An imprint of Ryland Peters & Small Ltd
20–21 Jockey's Fields, London WC1R 4BW
341 E 116th St, New York, NY 10029

www.rylandpeters.com

10 9 8 7 6 5 4 3 2 1

A CIP catalog record for this book is available from the Library of Congress and the British Library.

ISBN: 978-1-78249-711-0

Printed in China

Editor: Marion Paull
Designer: Emily Breen
Illustrators: Robyn Mclennan
and Dionne Kitching
Additional picture credits are on
page 144.

Commissioning editor: Kristine Pidkameny
Senior editor: Carmel Edmonds
Art director: Sally Powell
Production manager: Gordana Simakovic
Publishing manager: Penny Craig
Publisher: Cindy Richards

Important health note
Please be aware that the information contained in this book and the opinions of the author are not a substitute for medical attention from a qualified health professional. If you are suffering from any medical complaint or are worried about any aspect of your health, or if you are pregnant, please ask your doctor's advice before proceeding. The publisher and author can take no responsibility for any injury or illness resulting from the advice given or the techniques or postures demonstrated within this volume.

contents

introduction

We all move through life with the constant companion, the gift, of breath. We also spend much of our lives communicating, creating, and loving through our hands. Essential yet often overlooked, the breath and hands can be portals to self-discovery, healing, and inner peace. Although we age, fall ill, sustain injuries to the body, suffer heartbreak, loss, and mental disturbances, for as long as we are on this planet in our bodies, we have breath. Human beings, including very young children, people with physical limitations, and the elderly, all have access to breath and, in most cases, we have the ability to use our hands, which means there is never a time when using breath and mudras—yoga poses for your hands—isn't possible. That adds enormously to the ways in which we can use yoga,

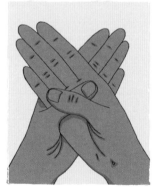

and for how long, and opens the door to many people to enjoy this ancient and transformative practice.

Yoga is my passion and it is a joy to know that we can tap into its science and magic in bite-sized morsels and derive myriad benefits in the same way that snacking on nutritious and tasty tidbits can provide important nutrients and keep our engines running beautifully. Even when we cannot, for one reason or another, sit down to a full three-course meal, we can still savor the flavor of communing with mind, body, and spirit.

I have taught yoga for almost two decades and practiced it for almost three. My personal practice can vary from a traditional one and a half to two-hour *asana* practice to a 20-minute meditation, depending on the day. Within that range there are two consistent and essential components for

me and they are what this book is about and what you hold in your hands right now. Without my practice, I would not be able to navigate the sometimes harsh terrain of the world in which we live. A little can go a long way and it's never too late or too early to tap into your inner light through yoga.

So for those who are still skeptical that they can practice *asanas* (yoga poses) or do not consider themselves the "yoga type" I ask you, do you breathe? Can you make a thumbs-up? If so, you can practice yoga here and now and elevate yourself on every level! No yoga outfit is necessary, no special strength or flexibility is a prerequisite, and there is nothing to lose but anxiety, pain, and mental clutter. What's to gain? Vitality, radiance, joy, clarity, and ease. You may be wondering how something as mundane (or is it?) as your breath and something as common and functional as your hands can

have such an effect. If you are curious, and since you have come this far already it seems you are, I am thrilled to take you on this journey.

The book is organized by condition that requires remedy and by desire that seeks to be fulfilled. It is meant for both the raw beginner and the seasoned practitioner or teacher. There is a breath and mudra practice for each condition and desire, as well as a combined practice with a "jewel thought" meditation. Feel free to peruse the book and see what calls out to you or to refer to the contents for a more specific approach. The magic and power of these ancient practices are now in your hands!

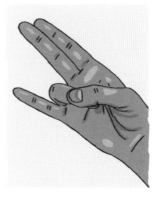

THE BASICS

CHAPTER 1
BREATH IS LIFE

breath: the power of breathing; life

also known as: life force, inspiration

The breath is like the sky, so omnipresent that we almost forget it's there until it does something astounding like change color before our eyes; or, when cloud spotting, we see a magical kingdom emerge and a horse seems to gallop right out of the cotton candy cloud it was nestled in; or when the crack of thunder and bolt of lightning snap us into the electric brilliance of the present moment. Then the sky is anything but background scenery. It becomes the main event and takes us by the force of its NOW energy into the eternal present. In between those moments, the sky holds our connection to life by providing a place for the sun, moon, and stars to hang and upon which we can plant the seeds of our dreams. The sky is like one of those clear plastic umbrellas that keeps us grounded and shielded from the overwhelming expanse that is space, yet it is also the window to the vastness of the cosmos and stimulates ponderings on the nature of existence. The sky has always been there, like our breath.

The breath is like the sky for its many unsung moments. There is no switch for either, they exist independently and yet it is by their existence that we can exist. From the first inhale, which could be called the inspiration to live, to our last exhale, which is the ultimate surrender and letting go, the breath is our companion.

As we grow, evolve, and explore the world, as we shift, change, and reinvent, as we love, lose, and love again, there is the breath.

When we turn our inner gaze upon our breath and begin to notice it, feel it, hear it, enjoy it, we experience life in a different way. On a physical level, yogic science says that we can improve the functioning of the body by cleansing the 72,000 energy channels or nadis. These channels of energy move our life force (*prana*) and when they are cleansed, they stay fluid and clear like a fresh, beautifully running river. When we practice pranayama (controlling the flow of breath), we are enriching our blood with more oxygen, which purifies the blood and supports healthy functioning of the respiratory system. Additionally, we fuel the burning of glucose. These actions produce energy, which gives power to the muscular contractions of the body. If we want to climb a mountain, we must consider our breathing capacity and our body must respond efficiently to give us the energy and strength required. If we want to relax, we can turn to the breath as well. It is a centerpiece to all that we are and all that we do and is connected to every aspect of human experience, yet we often don't think of it at all.

We live in a wonderful age of expansion and understanding where it is becoming widely recognized by traditional, functional, and alternative medical practitioners and healing specialists that breath practice can reduce anxiety and depression, lower stress levels, balance blood pressure, increase energy levels, improve sleep, and aid in pain management, among other benefits. Over the course of 25 years it has been my personal experience and observation that all of this and more is true.

On a spiritual level the breath, as with the sky, forges a bond with the unseen wonder of being alive. It is as basic to our experience as it gets—no breath no life—and yet it is ever mysterious. Where does the breath come from? It's a constant reminder of the divine-source energy force field in which we live and that we are ultimately not in charge. You may believe that breath is a gift from God, or that the unknown scientific mysteries of the universe have aligned in a way that gave you form and function, but we can all agree that without breath we do not exist and that each breath is a precious gift.

how to breathe

"Huh? Wait, don't I already know? I'm alive!" Yes, this is true and you have done a fine job so far. Now we will take it to the next level with pranayama. This is the control or manipulation of the breath to collaborate with the life force toward a particular goal. Now we go from survival to thrival! We take the gift of our own breath and direct it for our own purpose, be that to wake up, slow down, focus, or something else.

In this section of the book you will find a way to become aware of your breath plus ten more breath techniques to practice and use either on their own or with suggested mudras for each condition. The mudras are powerful and effective on their own but when combined with a breath technique, they can become supercharged.

I offer you both the English and the Sanskrit names for the breath techniques, but primarily refer to the English throughout. However, I encourage you to use what comes most naturally to you. Some may feel drawn to the Sanskrit while others may find the English easier to connect with. The main point is to keep it simple, practical, and joyful as you develop these new relationships.

WHAT TO DO WITH YOUR BODY WHILE YOU BREATHE

While you can breathe in any position as we do every day throughout our life, there are optimum positions for focused breath techniques. Whatever position you choose, it is most important that you are comfortable and relaxed.

Sitting

This can be in a chair or on the floor. If you are in a chair, make sure you have both feet on the ground and you are sitting upright and balanced.

    If you are on the floor, you can sit in cross-legged Easy Pose (*Sukhasana*), either flat on the ground or on a bolster or folded blanket so you are slightly elevated. If your hips or knees feel uncomfortable, I suggest a yoga block or rolled towels, blankets, or pillows, evenly placed under each outer knee.

    Another seated position is Thunderbolt Pose (*Vajrasana*). In this pose you rest on the shins with the tops of the feet on the floor and buttocks on heels. Your legs are together and your spine is straight. This pose stretches the legs and ankles and strengthens your spine. If your knees are uncomfortable, choose another position.

Standing

If practicing while standing, have both feet evenly placed on the ground, hip-width apart if possible, stomach slightly drawn in, tailbone descending, and spine tall and straight. This is a modified Mountain Pose (*Tadasana*).

Lying down

Lying down is fine for a few simple breath and mudra techniques but it is not the best position for many of them. The reason for this is that the main energy channel for the body (*Sushumna Nadi*) is best accessed when the spine is upright and straight. However, in a few cases I suggest you rest on the floor in Corpse Pose (*Savasana*), arms about 8 inches (20cm) from your body, palms facing up, and legs comfortably spread apart. Your whole body is in a relaxed state, free of muscular tension.

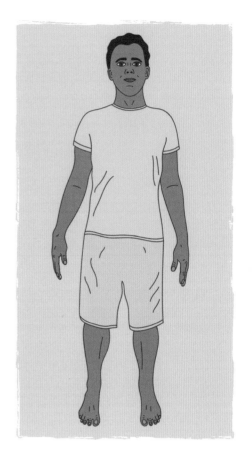

breath practices
ready, set, breathe

Get ready for a pranayama buffet! You can use this section to become familiar with the various breath practices that will be offered in the book and to explore and gain confidence with each of them. Please remember that, as with all aspects of yoga, it is important that this healing practice be approached free from judgment or tension. The breath affects and influences every cell in the body so a compassionate and patient approach is key for maximum benefits.

For timing, I refer mostly to "rounds" of breath and on occasion to number of minutes. A round is one inhale and one exhale. If practicing the breath on its own, a general rule of thumb is to start with 10–30 rounds, which will take around 1–3 minutes. You may close your eyes during the breath work or keep them open with a soft gaze fixed on one particular spot. In Sanskrit, this spot is called a *drishti*. Unless otherwise stated for certain breath practices, breathe in and out through your nose.

BREATH AWARENESS

Much like the title suggests, this is simply becoming aware of your breath and holding that attention on purpose.

Gently but firmly direct your attention, as many times as it takes, with patience, toward your breath. Feel the sensation of the breath in your body, wherever you notice it, as it comes and goes through your nose. You may find it helpful to direct your focus to a specific area, such as your belly or chest or nostrils. You do not need to alter your breath but simply observe your natural breathing and passively allow your thoughts to move along without attaching to any particular thought for any length of time. Instead attach your mind to your breath. This is a perfect way to begin to meditate.

EQUAL BREATH
(Sama Vritti Pranayama)

Aside from Breath Awareness, Equal Breath is the simplest of the breath techniques and is an excellent choice for stress reduction. It is a perfect breath for children and teens as well.

After a few moments of Breath Awareness, begin to count to four in your mind as you inhale through your nose, then pause briefly and count to four silently as you exhale through your nose.

TRIUMPHANT/VICTORIOUS BREATH
(Ujjayi Pranayama)

This breath practice, which is generally (and throughout this book) referred to by the Sanskrit name rather than the translation, builds upon Breath Awareness but adds sound and action to hold your attention more firmly to the breath and therefore the present moment. In this way, you "triumph" over the chatter of the mind. It is the most common breath used in a yoga class to help you to deepen your concentration and to achieve a greater mind-body connection. This can facilitate more depth, progress, and healing in the postures.

On your inhale "hug" or slightly constrict your throat so that it sounds like wind in a tunnel or "whoosh" and on your exhale, push the breath out through the same "hug" in the back of your throat. It should feel as if you are breathing in and out of a nose in your throat rather than your nostrils. These breaths are longer and deeper than your natural breath.

You may also combine *Ujjayi Breath* with Equal Breath by adding the count of four. This is especially helpful for those extra busy mind moments.

THREE-PART BREATH
(Dirga Pranayama)

Three-part Breath is stress relieving and grounding.

For this practice visualization is helpful. Imagine filling a glass of water from bottom to top as you fill yourself with breath. Inhale into the bottom of the belly, then your solar plexus, finishing the breath in your chest. Pause briefly when you have filled your glass and then exhale from the upper chest, solar plexus, and finally bottom of the belly as if you were pouring the water from the glass.

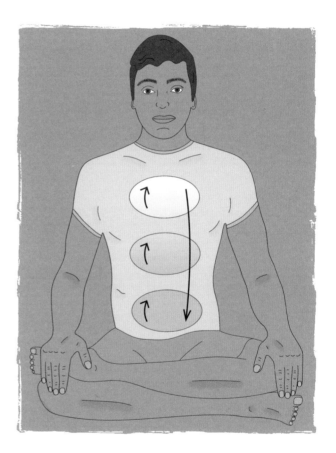

SUN BREATH
(Surya Bhedana Pranayama)

With this breathing technique, which is sometimes called Right Nostril Breathing, we invoke the energy of the sun. This breath can cultivate perseverance, enthusiasm, and zeal, and renew your hope.

From a seated position, place your left hand on your thigh. Fold the index and middle finger of your right hand into your palm leaving the thumb, ring finger, and pinky fingers free. (This is *Vishnu Mudra.*) You can do this with your left hand if you are left-handed. Close your left nostril with your ring finger and inhale through the right nostril. Then gently pinch both nostrils shut, using the thumb on the right nostril, and pause for a few seconds with both nostrils closed. Lift the ring finger from the left nostril and exhale through it. Continue so that you always inhale through the right and exhale through the left.

inhale . . .

exhale . . .

MOON BREATH
(Chandra Bhedana Pranayama)

This breathing technique, which is sometimes called Left Nostril Breathing, is cooling to the body and mind.

From a seated position, place your left hand on your thigh. Fold the index and middle finger of your right hand into your palm leaving the thumb, ring finger, and pinky fingers free. (This is *Vishnu Mudra.*) You can do this with your left hand if you are left-handed. Close your right nostril with your thumb and inhale through the left nostril. Then gently pinch both nostrils shut, using the ring finger on the left nostril, and pause for a few seconds with both nostrils closed. Lift the thumb from the right nostril and exhale through it. Continue so that you always inhale through the left and exhale through the right.

inhale . . .

exhale . . .

ALTERNATE NOSTRIL BREATH
(Nadi Shodhana Pranayama)

This pranayama technique clears the two main energy channels of the body and balances the hemispheres of the brain, which can result in greater energy and focus. It is sometimes called Sun/Moon Breath.

Sit comfortably and position your left hand, facing up or down on your leg. (If you prefer a mudra, touch the thumb to the index finger in *Jnana* or *Chin Mudra*—*Jnana* is facing up, *Chin* is facing down.) As with Sun Breath and Moon Breath, take *Vishnu Mudra*: fold the index and middle finger of your right hand into your palm leaving the thumb, ring finger, and pinky finger free. Close your right nostril with your thumb, and inhale deeply through your left nostril. At the top of your inhale place the ring finger of your right hand over your left nostril, gently pinching the nose and pausing the breath. Then release your thumb and exhale through the right nostril. Inhale through the right nostril, close both, and exhale through the left. This is one cycle or round.

inhale . . .

exhale . . .

inhale . . .

exhale . . .

BELLOWS BREATH *(Bhastrika Pranayama)*

This is a great energizer breath. It is best for beginners to practice Bellows Breath sitting down, but those who are more experienced in breathing practices could do it standing up. In kundalini yoga, it is even practiced in certain poses. This practice is not recommended during pregnancy or for those with hypertension or panic disorder. Substitute with *Ujjayi Breath* for 1–3 minutes.

To begin, take a few breaths in and out through your nose, noticing your belly expand on the inhale and contract on the exhale. Inhale a natural half-breath, then begin Bellows Breath by exhaling forcefully through your nose and inhaling at the same rate, which is quick—about one cycle per second. The inhale and exhale are even in tempo and intensity. Your body is still and straight except for the pumping action in your diaphragm. Begin with 10 rounds and rest for 3–5 natural breaths in between. Then work up to 20 rounds and then 30 rounds with the resting breaths in between. If you feel lightheaded or dizzy, relax and breathe naturally and stay with 10 pumps at a time for 3 rounds.

SKULL SHINING BREATH *(Kapalabhati Kriya)*

This technique is a kriya, which is a breath practice that is used for clearing, cleansing and purifying, and revitalizing. It is most commonly done seated although can also be done standing up. This practice is not recommended during pregnancy or for those with hypertension or panic disorder. Substitute with *Ujjayi Breath* for 1–3 minutes.

Place your hands on your belly or rest them on your legs. Inhale fully through your nose and exhale through your mouth. On your next inhale, stop short of a full breath and exhale through your nose with a forceful blow as your abdomen engages toward your navel. Let your inhale follow naturally. Focus on the exhale, which comes from the action of the belly pulling in. The inhale is a slower, natural reaction to the force of the exhale. Both breaths are done through the nose. It sounds a bit like a train chugging along or the piston of an engine. To start with, practice 3 rounds of 11 breaths with 2 or 3 natural breaths in between. You may eventually increase to 3 rounds of 27 breaths.

COOLING BREATH AND HISSING BREATH *(Sitali Pranayama and Sitkari Pranayama)*

Cooling Breath is a natural air conditioner that is perfect for cooling a temper or mitigating a hot flash.

Take a few deep breaths into your belly then form an "O" with your lips and slip your tongue through the opening, folding it to resemble a straw or tiny taquito. Wait until some saliva has formed and then breathe in through the "straw" (or bird's beak as the yogis saw it) drinking in the cool moisture. When you finish inhaling, close your lips and exhale completely through your nose. Continue with the breath for 3–5 minutes if possible.

If you are not genetically predisposed to form a straw with your tongue, you can practice Hissing Breath, which is exactly the same practice but with a variation on the tongue position. For Hissing Breath, gently press your teeth together and open your lips so your teeth are exposed. Your tongue is folded back so the underside presses the roof of your mouth, resembling a quesadilla. Draw the moistened air in through the sides of your mouth and exhale through the nose.

cooling breath

hissing breath

BEE BREATH *(Brahmari Pranayama)*

This is wonderful for relieving stress and sends a healing vibration through the vocal chords and chest. It can be practiced seated, on a chair or the floor, or lying down.

Place one hand on your heart and one hand on your belly. Inhale and as you exhale make a deep humming sound like a bee. Hum from the chest and belly more than from the lips. Let the "breath buzz" fade out naturally. Do not strain for the sound to last, rather let it softly and naturally fade in the way a buzz from a bee fades as it flies farther away from you.

THE BREATH CONNECTS

The breath is spirit or life force made tangible. When we feel and connect with the breath, we are in direct communication with the force that breathes us. We are dancing with divinity, and we become conscious of the rhythm of life. We all breathe the same breath. The wind carries our breaths and our spoken thoughts and words across the world. We are sharing the world with each other as we breathe.

When we consider this, we can begin to find the unity that is at the heart of yoga. We are united by the life force we share, and our words, whispers, and prayers can be carried by the wind to land gently on the shoulders and in the hearts and minds of all humanity.

CHAPTER 2
MUDRAS: YOU'VE GOT THE WHOLE WORLD IN YOUR HANDS

mudra: seal; any of the formal body positions and postures used in yoga and meditation

from *mud:* delight

and *ra:* to bring forth

Mudras are mainly positions that we take with our hands in the same way we use the body to take positions in yoga. Often, they are called the yoga of the hands. They also seal in a particular intention or focus for the body, mind, and spirit. There are whole body mudras as well, but this book focuses on hand mudras.

Our hands are extensions of the heart and as such they carry the spirit of what many (including yogic sages) say is the ultimate creative force of the universe—love. We communicate our thoughts and nourish our very cells through writing, drawing, music, painting, and cooking among other things. It is through touch that we connect with one another, sending messages of encouragement and comfort, support and sensitivity.

The hands are a universe of information and connected intimately to our emotions as they spontaneously tell the story of our feelings. Think of a small child suddenly clapping in delight, or an athlete happily shaking fists overhead after a winning play. As we talk, we gesture, dancing in and out of mudras, bringing more visual poetry to our stories and experience.

Mudras, like yoga, are ancient and can be found in many cultures. "Unofficial" mudras show up in our daily lives. Just watch politicians and newscasters using their hands to make a point. While driving you may have been on one side or the other of a few angry "mudras." We are always using the power of the hands to express. When we practice using our hands intentionally, we open the door to a powerful and magical world.

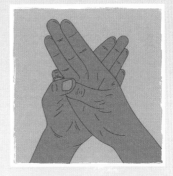

Throughout history, the magic and power of healing through the hands has been explored and experimented with, documented and depicted through palmistry, acupressure, ayurveda (Indian healing sister science to yoga), Chinese medicine, chakras, astrology, and reflexology. And, of course, mudras! What these practices have in common is the understanding that our hands, and especially our fingers, are like tiny universes and road maps to everything from our physical health to emotional state. We can affect our organs, muscles, moods, and more by the touch of our fingertips. So we truly hold the world of ourselves within our hands.

the elements and chakras in your hands

These diagrams show which fingers correspond to which element and which chakra, or energy center in the body. The elements are from the Indian healing art of ayurveda, which works on the premise that we are composed of the same elements as all of the natural world, and that we are at our healthiest when they are balanced. The chakras are particular areas in the body that correspond to the physical, emotional, and mental balance that relates to that area. In Sanskrit, chakra means "wheel," signifying that our life force is spinning inside us like a wheel of light. These diagrams may give you a more tangible idea of how your mudra practice taps into your whole being in such a powerful way.

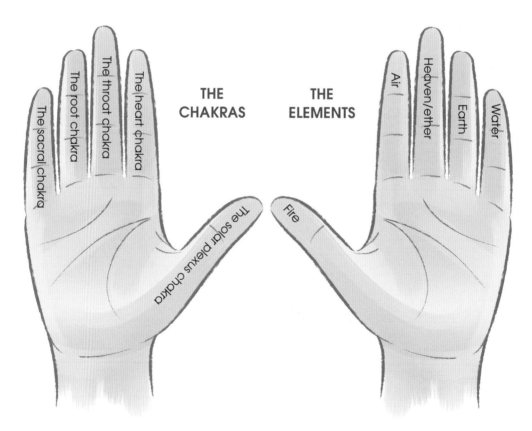

THE CHAKRAS

The sacral chakra
The root chakra
The throat chakra
The heart chakra
The solar plexus chakra

THE ELEMENTS

Air
Heaven/ether
Earth
Water
Fire

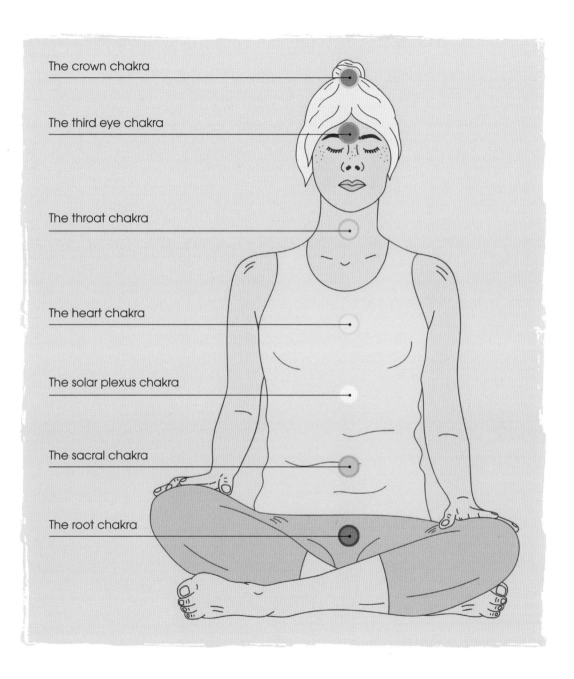

The crown chakra

The third eye chakra

The throat chakra

The heart chakra

The solar plexus chakra

The sacral chakra

The root chakra

hand reflexology maps

The hand reflexology maps will help you visualize and become acquainted with the reflex points or end points of the nadis (energy channels) that correspond to organs and muscles in the body. The mudras stimulate and balance these points through pressure and flexibility, which works with the

LEFT HAND REFLEXOLOGY POINTS

1 Spinal column

2 Uterus/prostate

3 Lumbar region

4 Bladder

5 Pancreas

6 Thyroid/parathyroid

7 Throat

8 Head

9 Neck

10 Stomach

11 Brain

12 Pineal gland

13 Pituitary gland

14 Eyes

15 Frontal and maxillary sinuses

16 Ears

17 Chest, lungs, and bronchial tubes

18 Solar plexus

19 Adrenal gland

20 Kidneys

21 Intestines

22 Arm and shoulder

23 Heart

24 Spleen

25 Hips and thighs

26 Ovaries/testes

27 Lymph

28 Sciatic nerve

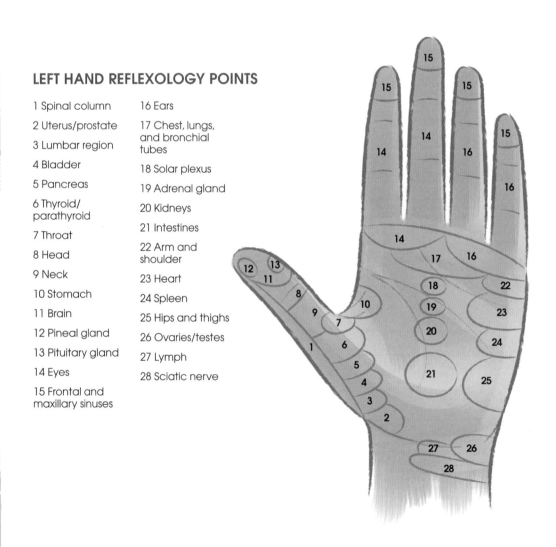

circulation of *prana* and blood flow. You can have fun experimenting with these reflexology points, which will increase your sensitivity and awareness for your mudra practice.

RIGHT HAND REFLEXOLOGY POINTS

1 Spinal column

2 Uterus/prostate

3 Lumbar region

4 Bladder

5 Pancreas

6 Thyroid/ parathyroid

7 Throat

8 Head

9 Neck

10 Stomach

11 Brain

12 Pineal gland

13 Pituitary gland

14 Eyes

15 Frontal and maxillary sinuses

16 Ears

17 Chest, lungs, and bronchial tubes

18 Solar plexus

19 Adrenal gland

20 Kidneys

21 Gallbladder

22 Liver

23 Intestines

24 Arm and shoulder

25 Hips and thighs

26 Ovaries/testes

27 Lymph

28 Sciatic nerve

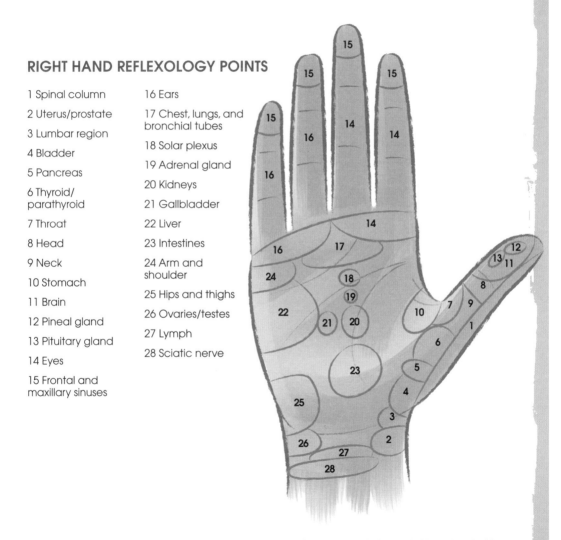

how to mudra

I love thinking of mudra as a verb. To mudra or not to mudra? Well, since it literally breaks down to "bring forth delight," I say you'll never go wrong with a mudra! So let's go over a few helpful hints to get the most from your mudras. We will refer to the mudras by their Sanskrit name as is the more common practice and because some don't have an English translation. Whenever possible the English will be provided.

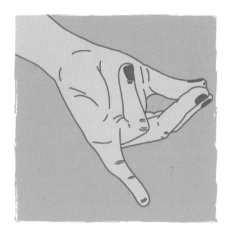

MUDRA PREP 101

Like any other part of the body, the hands will enjoy a little TLC before launching into a position, so ideally, and if possible, spend a few moments rubbing the hands together vigorously, wiggle the fingers or flick them, and circle your wrists a few times in each direction. This can loosen the joints, increase the circulation, and stimulate the nadis (energy channels) for an increased effect.

For body positions, refer to the section on "How to breathe" for sitting, standing, and lying down suggestions and instructions (page 14).

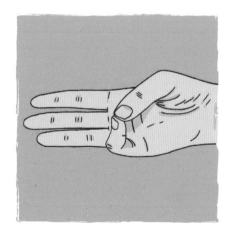

when to mudra

EMERGENCY MUDRAS

This is the prescription for on the spot mood adjustments. This is the anywhere, anytime protocol to help you through a challenging moment, improve your focus, de-escalate anxiety, ground you, provide a quick energy boost, and so on. In cases such as this you may find yourself holding a mudra at your desk, in the hospital, in the doctor's or dentist's office, on public transportation, at a family dinner, under the table at a board meeting, in a dressing room, before an interview, test, or audition, while waiting in line, or anywhere else you may find yourself. You can carry this book with you for just such moments, or you may wish to familiarize yourself with a few "go to" mudras. With this style of mudra practice we are simply employing an excellent tool as a reminder that while we may not have control of the events outside of ourselves, we do have choices about how we react. A well-placed mudra has gotten me through many a sticky wicket, and preserved my composure during times of duress.

If possible, hold the mudra for a minimum of 3 minutes with your attention in the present.

INTUITIVE MUDRAS

With these mudras, you are focusing on tuning in and centering yourself. Set aside time to practice. You may have an intention you want to concentrate on that day or perhaps over the course of some time. You can scroll through the book and choose what appeals to you in relation to this intention or a theme you are drawn toward, or you can tune in and do an internal check kindly asking your higher self, "What do I need today?" Or "Please guide me to choose the perfect mudra for this present moment." Then find the practice in the book that best suits your answer. You can even play with a more random intuitive style by simply opening the book, letting yourself be led to a page, taking that mudra, and seeing what comes! This way of working with mudras is fun, playful, and helps to develop your intuition while creating a more dynamic dialogue between your body, mind, and soul.

For these mudras, I suggest holding for a minimum of 3 minutes up to 30 minutes once or twice a day, or follow the instructions in the chosen section of the book that correspond to the breaths.

THERAPEUTIC MUDRAS

For chronic or severe conditions, you will reap greater benefits if you approach the mudras with a healthy dose of discipline and think of them as natural medicine.

Begin by holding the mudras for 3 minutes minimum, several times a day. Then, as your hands adjust and grow stronger and more flexible, you may find you can move to 3 times per day for 15 minutes.

If possible for you, you may work your way up to holding the mudras for 45 minutes at a stretch. This may seem like a lot (and it is!) so don't fret if that's not possible. More important than getting to such a long hold is a frequent and consistent practice for the full therapeutic benefits to kick in, especially with more challenging conditions. For example, if you have chronic digestive issues and want to use the mudra as part of your healing plan, I suggest one of the timetables above on a regular and consistent basis. For temporary acute conditions, such as headaches or sinus trouble, follow the same pattern and discontinue when your symptoms have gone.

For mudras to produce a desired physical or mental effect, such as healthy skin, improved fertility, or a boost in confidence, practice anywhere between 3 and 30 minutes 1–4 times per day until your desired effect has been achieved.

Natural healing is often a bit more labor intensive than conventional treatments but comes without any nasty side effects and has multiple positive side benefits. Like inner peace!

MUDRAS AND MEDITATION

Mudras are extremely helpful in beginning or maintaining a meditation practice (see page 38). In addition to the many benefits the mudras provide, they act as an anchor for the restless mind, tethering it into the moment in order to hold the mudra. It is not necessary to meditate formally while practicing mudras but you may find that you drop into a state of mindfulness with less mental effort when including the mudras.

DAILY MUDRAS

In addition to the circumstances already described, I always suggest a morning and/or night practice for all aspects of yoga and especially for breath practices, mudras, and meditation.

Morning mudra

In the morning, we have cleared our emotional palette, released mental momentum, rested the body, and have a sense of rebirth. It's the perfect time to create a positive vibration by holding your attention on an intention that aligns your body, mind, and spirit to energetically design your day. A 10–20-minute breath and mudra practice in the morning will have a powerful and lasting effect throughout the day.

Nighttime mudra

A few serene and reflective moments at the end of the day can cleanse and cure a million small ills. I highly recommend a 10–20-minute practice of chosen breath and mudra that appeals to you, offering up your day and letting go. The sweet moments will linger, the challenges be muted or handed over to the higher power for the night, and some grateful reflection can bring order to chaos. This ritual can make the difference between a deep peaceful sleep or a restless night still wrestling the demons of the day.

mudras featured in this book

There are a huge number of mudras, but the ones featured in this book and referenced in the conditions part of this book are listed below.

meditation guiding your mind with jewel thoughts

In Hindu and Buddhist texts, as well as various spiritual literature sources, references to the jewel in the lotus are accepted as signifying human divinity (the jewel) within the cosmos (the lotus flower). Although the practice of yoga itself requires no religious or spiritual affiliation, and can be practiced by anyone of any background, it is by nature spiritual in that it serves as a path to enlightenment.

What is enlightenment? Well, what it is not is the attachment to suffering. Enlightenment can be explained by the state of consciousness, or "beingness," in which we are aware and sensitive to the suffering, pain, and hardships of being human but live in a state of inner peace and bliss. We are not removed from our pain, or that of the world, but we are able to contain and feel all aspects of the human experience while still being anchored in love, peace, and joy. This book is like an anchor to ground you in the present moment, and an offering to your highest state of awareness where peace, love, and joy are always present.

With every breath I feel my mind, body and

The jewel thoughts are the affirmative gems that nestle at the heart of each practice. They are the consolidated essence of each condition in its simplest, pure, positive form. You may discover that you resonate with them or you don't. You may find that they stimulate the desire to hatch your own jewel thought! If you choose to use them, I suggest that you place the book in front of you while you practice and refer to the jewel thought as offered in each section or as you intuitively feel it best accompanies your mudra and breath. There is no "right" way to do this—just a chance to connect within and without and let the words guide and uplift you.

If this is too vague for comfort, you can take a more concentrated approach by repeating the jewel thought silently or out loud until you have it firmly in your mind, before adding in the breath practice. You can also leave the book open and read it to yourself while breathing with the mudra. The most essential component is that you allow yourself to truly feel the thought and to embrace its essence and meaning, more than to recite it perfectly in your mind.

soul reawaken. I am alive with possibility.

CONDITIONS AND REMEDIES

CHAPTER 3
BREATHING AND MUDRAS FOR THE BODY

Both breath and mudras can benefit a variety of physical problems we may have—not just joint pain and carpal tunnel, which affect the hands and wrists, but also those which affect our organs, such as our heart and lungs, and issues which have an impact on our well-being, such as insomnia or fertility.

eye conditions
beauty is in the eye ...

There's nothing like a road trip to open our eyes to the bizarre and beautiful landscape of our world. We watch the terrain morph and shapeshift, as our eyes gaze upon the variety of texture, color, and design. We drink in the gorgeous perfection of nature and see marks of the audacious, precocious human imprint through the windshield as through the windows to our soul.

There's also nothing like getting lost (or found!) in the world of a good book to remind us that our imaginations know no limits and our willing suspension of disbelief is firmly intact, when we find the right match of author and story. But if the windshield is dirty and bug laden, our glasses are scratched and smudged, the experience is as mottled as the glass. Eyes are the unsung heroes in work and play. In our current lifestyle, they are overworked and underpaid.

Long hours spent in a fixed stare at artificially lighted screens, both big and small, was not part of the original design. Our eyes are meant to move frequently, shifting focus from near to far. They are happiest when they are well hydrated, get plenty of rest, and perhaps when they are crinkling at the corners as a consequence of a good laugh. If we want to see the beauty while enjoying our work and creative lives more, we must remember to nurture those precious "beholders."

If you experience neck and shoulder pain, headaches, blurred vision, or feel generally exhausted despite being rested, you may be suffering from eyestrain. In addition to keeping your computer at arm's length, glasses and screens clean, taking breaks every 20 minutes, and blinking frequently, this mudra and breath practice are sure to refresh your eyes and reveal more beauty and interest in your world.

SKULL SHINING BREATH WITH PALMING

Among the many benefits of Skull Shining Breath are improved circulation and blood flow to the eyes. It can help release accumulated pressure in the optic nerves and stimulate the life force, which can strengthen and brighten the eyes.

If you wish to practice the breath on its own, choose your seated position (page 15) and begin the first of 3 rounds of Skull Shining Breath (page 23). If you plan to add the mudra, practice one round of the breath and then begin palming by rubbing your hands together vigorously and cupping them over your eyes with space between palms and eyelids. Breathe deep and slow. Relax your eyes into the warm, healing energy of your hands, bathing the eye sockets in your breath. Make sure your hands block out the light and are not pressing on your eyes. Now add the mudra on the following page.

This practice is not recommended during pregnancy or for those with hypertension or panic disorder. Instead, follow instructions for *Ujjayi Breath* for 1–3 minutes.

SUPER POWER EYESIGHT

Our two eyes show us the physical world. In yoga, the third eye is the place through which we can connect with the unseen world that is within us and also more than us. Skull Shining Breath not only nourishes the physical being, but also provides a clear channel that we can tune into for guidance. By practicing this breath and stimulating the third eye (pituitary gland), we cleanse this channel and come to "see" more clearly the bounty of wisdom that cannot be seen through our eyes alone. This is like a super power of epic proportions.

PRAN MUDRA *(Life-force Mudra)*

This powerhouse mudra has many applications but I find it especially useful for improving eyesight and soothing tired eyes. The power of touching earth, water, and fire points (page 28) activates the prana in an electric way; the extension of the air and ether fingers brings a spacious relaxing sensation to the eyes.

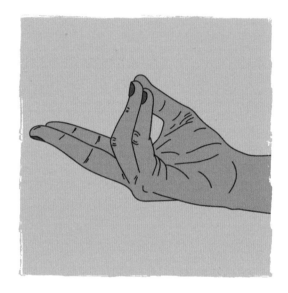

- Touch your thumbs to your ring and pinky fingers on both hands.
- Extend your middle and index fingers, keeping them together.
- Place the hands, palms up, on your thighs.
- Begin Skull Shining Breath.
- Between each round of breath, release *Pran Mudra* and rub the hands vigorously together for about 30 seconds, then cup them over your eyes.
- If adding the jewel thought below, do so while the hands are cupping the eyes.

I see the world through bright, clear eyes.
I see beauty inside and out.

JEWEL THOUGHT

ear trouble and motion sickness
hear and heal

When our hearing is temporarily impaired through infection, injury, or excess fluid, we can feel lost and disconnected, ungrounded and without center. There's the sensation of isolation or "being in a fishbowl." If the ear trouble is tinnitus (ringing in the ears), it may also feel as though we have to work through a sound barrier to communicate and relating to others is a struggle. We may long for quiet and inner peace and can't escape the noise of our own head. Imagine being relieved to be home, looking forward to kicking off your shoes and relaxing only to remember you can't because there's construction going on—and it's in your own head!

Interestingly, the physiology of motion sickness is thought to occur from this same experience of losing grounding or bearings because the inner ear perceives motion that the eyes don't register in the same way.

The ears are intimately connected with our sense of inner peace and balance in body and soul. When we feel disoriented, not at home in ourselves, have ear trouble, pain, or nausea, we can turn to *Shunya Mudra*, also called Sky Mudra or Heaven Mudra. This mudra is said to allow us to connect with *anahata*, which is the Sanskrit name for the heart chakra, meaning the "unstruck, unhurt, unbeaten" sound, the vibration of the celestial realm, which is serenity, peace, and balance. The heart chakra is located in the physical center of the body, with three main chakras above and three below, and is our emotional inner compass. This center governs the balance of giving and receiving and the idea that "home is where the heart is" or home is where there is love.

Ear issues and motion sickness are related to a sense of losing your emotional and physical center, so let's tune into *Shunya Mudra* and find a little heaven on earth.

BREATH AWARENESS WITH KUMBHAKA RETENTION

We will use the natural breath with Breath Awareness (page 17) and add a little twist. After a few moments of settling into the present and becoming aware of your breath, add a silent count in your mind—inhale to the count of 3, hold the breath for 3 (this is *Kumbhaka* or retention on the inhale) and then exhale to the count of 3. If you are going to use the mudra below, take the position with your hands now, and then practice 15–30 rounds, or until you feel a sense of peace and/or your nausea has decreased.

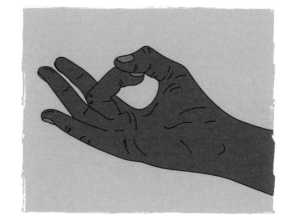

SHUNYA MUDRA *(Sky or Heaven Mudra)*

This mudra works with ether and space, the elements of the heart center.

- Bend your middle finger on each hand into the base of your thumb.
- Fold your thumb over the middle finger and gently press it down.
- Extend the index, ring, and pinky fingers.
- Place your hands, palms up, on your thighs.

I feel at home in my heart. I am tuned to the vibration of love. I am earth and sky.

JEWEL THOUGHT

sleep easy like a baby

To sleep is to surrender the day, restore and reboot, to float in a field of dreams and imagination, to experience catharsis and release and emerge born again to the gift of a new day. For many people, though, it is a wrestling match where body, mind, and sheets are tangled up in the future and the past, a time when the monsters in the recesses of the mind, having waited for the body to slow down and momentum to subside, pounce! Tragically, this often occurs right as we dare to let our defenses down and relax. If you are even occasionally in the latter scenario, it's hard not to envy the sleep of a baby, or a dog for that matter!

Sleep is on the top of the heap of what we need to be healthy and to perform at optimum levels. Although some people who are chronically sleep deprived may be high functioning, for most of us moods, focus, and overall joy factor are negatively affected by persistent lack of sleep. It doesn't take a doctor to diagnose (although you can find bushels of them who agree) that sleep deprivation is a serious health concern and a growing global problem. Technology, caffeine abuse, the pace of the world, financial concerns, illness, and anxiety are a few of the thieves in the night that come to steal our slumber.

So what do babies and dogs know that we don't? Or maybe it's what they don't know! They don't have jobs, children to take care of, world peace to worry about, and saving the environment on their minds. Could it be possible to get back to this state of inner freedom when we live such complicated lives? Yes! But to taste the freedom we have to prepare the mind and body. A little sleep hygiene (see box overleaf) can create the right conditions to pave the way from the stress response of the sympathetic nervous system to the sweet zone of relaxation—the parasympathetic nervous system.

SLEEP HYGIENE

Here are a few ways to soothe the savage nighttime beasties and get a good night's rest. I suggest testing this prescription for a week at least.

- *No screens 30 minutes to one hour before bed. Instead, read something uplifting or very tedious and boring—no news!*
- *Keep the lights low.*
- *Take a bath.*
- *Use essential oils, such as lavender, on the bottoms of your feet.*
- *Drink chamomile tea or golden milk (see recipe on page 140) 30 minutes before bed.*
- *Keep the window slightly open for air circulation.*
- *Keep a gratitude journal at your bedside.*

BEE BREATH

If you usually have trouble falling asleep, try the Bee Breath (page 25) sitting up in bed or on the floor next to your bed sitting in Easy Pose (page 15). You can put your index fingers in your ears with your elbows pointing down as this version is especially helpful for sleep trouble. Practice 5–10 rounds.

SHAKTI MUDRA *(Empowerment Mudra)*

This mudra evoking the goddess Shakti is my favorite sleep mudra, especially when I wake up in the night. It can be practiced seated with Bee Breath before sleep, or lying down with simple Breath Awareness for waking in the night.

- Hold your hands palms facing each other at chest height.
- Fold your thumbs into your palms.
- Wrap your index and middle fingers over your thumbs.
- Press the tips of your ring and pinky fingers together and press the folded middle and index fingers into each other.
- If practicing seated, hold the mudra with your hands in front of and slightly away from your chest. If lying down, hold the mudra with your hands touching your chest. Use Bee Breath or breathe naturally and slowly as appropriate for however long you need until you begin to feel drowsy.

headache calm the monkey

When I first met my husband, he had a wonderfully funny and disturbing piece of art that I came to appreciate more and more through the years. It was of a man holding his screaming head in front of himself as he chased it with the clear intent to shut himself up. I know that's a rather violent image for a book on harmony and healing, but if we are to be perfectly honest, there are times when we might feel quite desperate to find the off switch. This may be due to the consistent litany of thoughts (mostly useless and disruptive) that are commonly called "the monkey mind" or to dull the physical pain in the head. Often the headache comes from the pressure of too many thoughts, which can cause tension in the neck, jaw, and connective tissue covering the skull, which in turn creates an unpleasant squeezing sensation—also known as a headache!

When we have a headache, it is almost impossible not to think about it. In another area of the body we may be able to compartmentalize the pain somewhat while we focus on work, read something interesting, do something enjoyable, or otherwise engage our attention. But since the head is the container for the brain and therefore home to our thoughts and perceptions, if it aches, it's like trying to think through the pain when the pain is where the thinking process lives. It can feel a bit like wiping off your glasses with Vaseline to see better—not likely to work. What is more likely to be successful is to enter a state of relaxation in which the pressure and tension build-up may retreat and the healing life force called prana can flow.

Some of the many causes of headaches are anxiety, computer screen glare, noise, dehydration, eating and sleeping patterns, exercising too hard, not exercising enough, reactions to medications, poor posture, hormonal fluctuations, food sensitivities, and stress. Any one of these may result in poor circulation of blood and oxygen to the brain. This is where breath and mudras can come to the rescue before you find yourself chasing your head in circles!

ALTERNATE NOSTRIL BREATH

This breath is a wonderful way to balance, refresh, and relieve tension (page 22). After doing a few rounds you can add the mudra below with your free hand and continue the breathing practice for 10–30 rounds. You may wish to switch to both hands for the mudra, in which case practice with *Ujjayi Breath* (page 18) for 5–30 rounds.

MAHASIRS MUDRA *(Large Head Mudra)*

This mudra works wonders for headaches and when combined with one of the two soothing breath practices mentioned, you might make this your new over-the-counter headache cure!

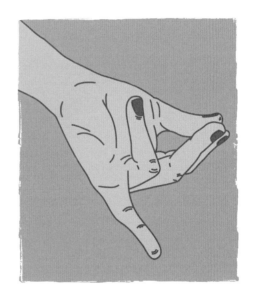

- Touch your thumb, index, and middle fingers together.
- Fold your ring finger into your palm.
- Extend your pinky finger.
- Either do this with your free hand or both hands and rest the hands, palms up, on your thighs or knees.

I release all tension in body and mind.
My mind is open and free. I am free.

JEWEL THOUGHT

healthy brain memory boost

There's nothing more frustrating or concerning than desperately grasping for a thought, song title, friend's name, or location of an item. "Senior moments" at any age can set off alarm bells. Many important lifestyle choices beside other components contribute to a healthy brain with a youthful memory, but quite often we are mentally oversaturated from the vast and ceaseless amount of information that we are privy to. If you are simply on overload, you may be easily distracted by every shiny or rusty thought in the constant parade through your mind. If this is the case, a lot can be gained (or recovered!) by taking a moment to BE in the moment. It is said that we have about 60,000 thoughts per day. You can bet that a very big portion of those thoughts are useless at best and often harmful and self-defeating. A yogic term in Sanskrit that speaks of this condition is *Citta Vritti*—mind chatter or monkey mind. I think of it as monkeys chattering loudly in my mind. Just imagine sitting in a room filled with dozens of loudly chattering monkeys and trying to remember anything at all! With this high-energy, high-volume mind condition, the thoughts we are searching for, such as high-caliber, creative, problem-solving, uplifting ones, can get buried in the hay like the proverbial needle.

If you are trying to remember where you put the needle in the haystack, the best thing to do is remove the hay. So, with this mudra, we are removing the "hay" by releasing mental clutter and trusting that the "needle" or whatever it is we want to remember will be revealed effortlessly. This will also be useful in quieting the mind so that our true genius can reveal itself.

My mind is clear and open like the sky.
All that I need to remember reveals itself
to me effortlessly.

JEWEL THOUGHT

BREATH AWARENESS OR UJJAYI BREATH

Choose from either Breath Awareness to calm and settle yourself, or *Ujjayi* to triumph over the cacophony of your busy brain.

Then come into a comfortable seated position either on the floor or in a chair. Follow the instructions for Breath Awareness (page 17) or *Ujjayi Breath* (page 18) for 10 rounds to center yourself. You can continue with just the breath practice or add in *Buchari Mudra* as well.

BUCHARI MUDRA *(Gazing into the Void)*

Sit in a comfortable position in front of a blank wall, preferably white in color.

- Place the thumb of your right hand in the space between your nose and upper lip.
- Fold your fingers into your palm except for your pinky, which should point up.
- Set your gaze onto the tip of your pinky and breathe deep and slow using either Breath Awareness or *Ujjayi Breath*.

- Hold the posture for 10–30 rounds of breath. Then release the mudra but continue to gaze at the exact spot on the wall where your pinky was and concentrate only on that spot for at least a minute or 10–12 breaths. If you want to include the jewel thought, add it now and stay with a soft focused gaze for as long as you want to.

sinus trouble smell the roses

This is something I actually do—and hope you do, too—especially when I'm in a hurry or feel short on time. I force myself to stop and smell a rose if there is one nearby. I almost never pass up the chance. It reminds us that the sweet life is right there waiting and the scent of roses is that of miracles and unconditional love. I'm definitely olfactory obsessed and need my essential oils to waft fragrances, the way a bee needs a flower.

When we experience temporary or chronic anosmia (loss of the sense of smell) our quality of life can be severely diminished. The olfactory sense is closely linked to memory, comfort, joy, and even our sense of safety. It may not be as bright and shiny as the other fab four senses, but it can definitely leave a void. That's not even to mention the discomfort and pressure of sinus headaches due to inflammation in the tissue lining of the mucous membranes!

Suffice it to say, whatever the reason, when our sinuses are clogged, so are we. When the sweet surrender of stopping for a flower or inhaling the aroma of our favorite dish eludes us, life can be a little flat. We may also experience brain fog and facial pain, feel sluggish and isolated, and lose our appetites or enjoyment of food. Sinus trouble can stem from a cold, allergies, environmental sensitivities, swimming, flying, dry air, a deviated septum, or reaction to medication and cancer treatments to name a handful of causes but not all. Fortunately, I have found great relief with, you guessed it, mudras!

Although it may sound counterintuitive to practice breathing when you can't even get a decent regular breath of air, quite often the right breath will do the trick in dislodging the fortress in your nose. We will elicit the healing power of water with *Varuna Mudra*, which works to increase the flow and hydrate us physically and emotionally. This coupled with Skull Shining Breath will bring light and movement. Stress and overly busy lives can make us more susceptible to sinus trouble in all its forms so let's pause and get busy smelling the roses once again.

SKULL SHINING BREATH

Once seated comfortably, with tissue on hand, practice a round of Skull Shining Breath (page 23). Then pause to incorporate the mudra below. Now do 3 rounds of the breath with the mudra. Pause between each round and hold the breath in for 8–15 seconds before exhaling completely and beginning the next round.

This practice is not recommended during pregnancy or for those with hypertension or panic disorder. Instead, follow instructions for *Ujjayi Breath* for 1–3 minutes.

VARUNA MUDRA *(God of Water Mudra)*

- Fold the pinky finger of the right hand into the palm.
- Hold the pinky with the thumb of the right hand.
- Place the right hand palm up, in the palm of the left, elbows bent.
- Gently press the thumb of the left hand onto the right thumb, holding the index, middle, and ring fingers (plus left-hand pinky) together on both hands.
- Hold your hands in front of your heart or rest them in your lap.

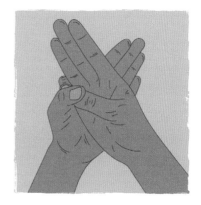

I release, dissolve, and surrender to the flow of life.

JEWEL THOUGHT

healthy skin **detox and glow**

Your skin is the one outfit you can never change, and yet your skin changes constantly throughout your life. It's the town crier of life's passages. "Here comes puberty!" Then "Crow's feet at 3 and 9 o'clock!" And of course, "All hail menopause and the great drought!" Skin is also not great at keeping secrets, such as lack of sleep, too many cocktails, or poor hydration hygiene. This beautifully crafted birthday suit is the spiritual gift that keeps on giving, as it can be a lesson in self-acceptance and the celebration of our individuality.

I learned a lot about this as a little girl, watching freckles appear like stars in a mountain sky throughout my childhood. I am a big fan of freckles on others and always have been but, in all honesty, as they sprouted upon my person at a rapid and aggressive rate during my formative years, they seemed to be more like a hostile takeover than angel kisses. That rocky relationship required nurturing. People who had smooth, freckle-free skin seemed to lead less complicated lives, as if somehow they had less to deal with. Ironically, by the time I came to appreciate the beauty of my freckles and all they taught me about self-love, the many faces of beauty, and acceptance—my wrinkles had infiltrated and the process started again.

From where I stand now, I love my skin not only for all it has taught me (including that skin has the power not only to divide people, but also to cause us to judge ourselves in a way that is damaging and divisive), but also for what it does. One avenue toward a healthier relationship with your skin is to focus on its multiple and essential purposes (see box opposite).

We can use breath and mudras to enhance the health and beauty of the skin and release limiting beliefs. Bellows Breath aids in digestion and detoxification through the skin and a version of the God of Water Mudra helps to maintain healthy hydration in the body. Together they provide a gorgeous glow that surpasses any perceived flaws as your breath cleans and balances the whole organism.

WHAT SKIN DOES

- *It keeps our bodies together so we aren't oozing blobs of consciousness but instead have a little decorum!*
- *It regulates our temperature and protects us from germs, toxins, and the elements.*
- *Perhaps one of the best things, but least considered, is that it gives us sensation. Our skin allows us to FEEL.*
- *Through skin we absorb the things we need and secrete the things we need to get rid of from the body.*

BELLOWS BREATH

Follow the instructions on page 23, or, if you are pregnant, or feel dizzy or unwell, skip this breath and practice Alternate Nostril Breath from page 22. Practice one round before adding the mudra on the following page, if using. Continue with 3 sets of Bellows Breath or 10–30 rounds of Alternate Nostril Breath.

To touch and be touched is the sweet gift of the skin

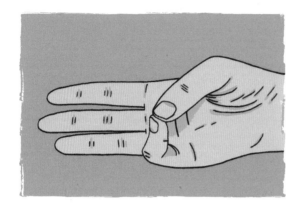

VARUN MUDRA *(God of Water Mudra)*

This is a variation of *Varuna Mudra* used for the sinuses.

- On each hand touch the thumb to the pad of the pinky finger, which balances the fire element in the thumb with the water element of the pinky finger.
- Place your hands, palms up, on your thighs.
- If you are practicing Alternate Nostril Breath, use one hand for *Varun Mudra* and the other for your breath.

I embrace myself. I am radiant and glowing in perfect balance with all that is.

JEWEL THOUGHT

heart health massage the muscle

The heart is the central point for so much of what it means to be human. We can't live without a heart and we don't really live without love. Not fully. By love I mean any kind of love—familial, romantic, spiritual, friendship love, love for animals, and so on.

The pumping action of the heart keeps the circulatory system fresh and operational. Blood flowing in and out of the heart is the physical counterpart of giving and receiving love, the circulation of life force that bathes us in oxytocin and smiles. The heart chakra (*anahata*) is the center through which we experience feelings of love and the sharing of them. It's also the center of our immune system and the thymus gland. By taking good care of your big beautiful ticker, you boost not only the quality and longevity of your physical life, but also your ability to live in a state of being in love with life. An imbalance in your physical heart may lead to coronary heart disease, heart attack, and coronary artery disease among other illnesses. An imbalance in your heart chakra can produce lung problems, heart problems, depressions, loneliness, excessive fear, and a judgmental nature.

According to studies led by John Cacioppo of the University of Chicago and Steve Cole from UCLA, "those who are socially isolated suffer from higher all-cause mortality, and higher rates of cancer, infection, and heart disease." Loneliness, which we could characterize as being without social connections, interactions, and loving exchanges, wreaks havoc on the immune system, sleep patterns, and as Cacioppo goes on to say, "can push blood pressure up into the danger zone for heart attacks and strokes. It undermines regulation of the circulatory system so that the heart muscle works harder and the blood vessels are subject to damage by blood flow turbulence." If there was ever a case for love being all you need, there it is. Well, that and a healthy diet, plenty of exercise and, of course, breathing and hand yoga. In addition to sending some loving appreciation to our own hearts, we can fine tune our sensitivity and reach out to those around us as often as possible. It's win/win in matters of the heart—giver and receiver both benefit. Truly, we are all in this together.

EQUAL BREATH

One of the main qualities of the heart chakra is balance, which makes Equal Breath a perfect choice here (page 18). If using the mudra below, practice one round of Equal Breath first, add the mudra, and then return to the breath for 10–30 rounds.

APAN VAYU MUDRA *(Downward Flow)*

This mudra has been called the "lifesaver" and is even used as first aid during a heart attack. It decreases the air element (which is the element of the heart chakra) and increases the earth element, which restores balance to the heart.

- Bring your index finger on each hand into the base of your thumb.
- Touch your thumbs to your middle and ring fingers on each hand.
- Extend the pinky fingers.
- Place the hands, palms up, on your thighs.

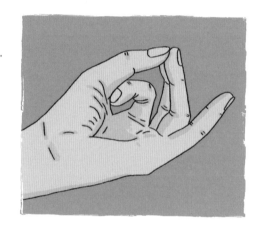

My heart is at ease. I am connected to all that is.

JEWEL THOUGHT

digestion
light your fire, cool your jets

Sometimes it's hard enough to have one brain, let alone two, and yet the belly is often called the "second brain." This relates to the important and popular topic of digestion. The brain and the gut are married, for better or worse, and their effect on each other runs both ways and quickly. Thoughts and feelings travel in the fast lane to and from the brain and gut, but not without taking a toll. (It's best to have a sense of humor about these things.) The gastrointestinal (GI) tract is especially sensitive to our emotions connected to past, present, and future. Our language reinforces the physical sensations arriving from thoughts and feelings—"gut wrenching," "butterflies," "knots," "somersaults," "feeling nauseous." Digestive juices can even be released at the mere mention of a tantalizing meal hovering on the horizon. The connection that runs from brain to belly is clear. In reverse, dealing with GI issues most certainly can be depressing and produce anxiety and stress as we navigate pain, discomfort, and even bathroom schedules to accommodate this rollercoaster relationship. So whichever the genesis, chicken or egg, stomach or brain, we may need some guidance to find peace. But what is causing this connection?

It is now widely understood among doctors, nutritionists, and scientists that having the right balance of healthy bacteria in your gut plays a key role in the healthy functioning of your GI tract, and your overall level of health and well-being. When under chronic stress due to any number of factors, including loss of loved ones, illness, financial issues, chronic anxiety, depression, panic disorder, mood disorders, addiction to name but a few, the fact is that our personal microbiome (collection of bacteria) does not function at top level.

According to Webster's Dictionary: "We depend on a vast army of microbes to stay alive; a microbiome that protects us against germs, breaks down food to release energy, and produces vitamins." Even generic daily stress can disturb the peace over time, as 80% of our immune system is located in the gut. When your system feels under siege, it can impact blood flow to your GI tract and the amount and type of good gut flora available.

Here's the kicker—healthy bacteria regulate cortisol (the stress hormone) and if they are compromised, the cortisol can run amuck. As in any heated situation, this can cause inflammation. Inflammation means things are not working in unison or harmony—there is too much of something, which causes upset and imbalance. Enter yoga, which happens to mean union, to bring things together (mind, body, and spirit/breath) and create a harmonious flow when we can allow our feelings to be heard without judgment and our bodies to relax into the NOW, stimulating healthy digestion on all levels.

For this practice we balance the hot and cool to create the perfect climate for peace in body and mind.

EQUAL BREATH

We turn to Equal Breath (page 18) to restore union and achieve balance. Lie on your back with your legs extended or bent at the knees with your feet on the ground. After one round of the breath, add the mudra opposite, if using, and do 4 rounds of the breath before relaxing your arms out to the sides at shoulder height for a few moments of natural breathing. Take up the mudra again, do another 4 rounds, and rest. Continue for as long as you like.

GARUDA MUDRA
(Mythological Bird—Half Human, Half Eagle)

This mudra works with the thumbs for the fire element, and lying down brings a cool quality. If you are experiencing acid reflux, it is preferable to sit up. You will still get the benefits without added agitation.

- Hold your hands in front of your chest, palms facing you.
- Cross your wrists and then press the pads of the thumbs firmly into each other. It doesn't matter which hand is nearer to your body.
- Fan the rest of your fingers out like bird wings.

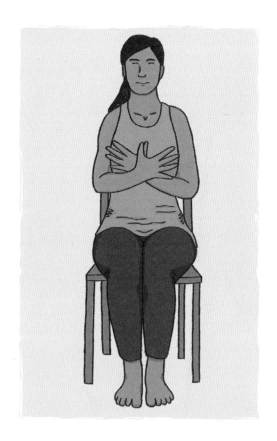

Like a bird, I spread my wings. I feel free and at peace in this moment.

JEWEL THOUGHT

respiratory conditions
love your lungs

This breath and mudra can be used to address numerous lung issues from minor colds to asthma, bronchitis and more, or as a daily practice for healthy lungs. Lung ailments, whether chronic or temporary, have many, varying causes including exposure to pollutants, allergies, and multiple chemical sensitivity (MCS), and some people are more predisposed to them than others.

One aspect not to be overlooked is the mind-body connection. If breath is life, the lungs are the sacred chambers where our feelings about life dwell. When the lungs are out of balance, it may be a result of fear of life, grief, depression, small hurts, or feelings of being overwhelmed. The lungs and heart are roommates, and therefore the emotions that relate to the heart chakra (unconditional love, balance, harmony, courage) can be "picked up" by the lungs and, when there is an imbalance, manifest into various respiratory ailments.

Inhalation is connected to inspiration, as in the inspiration to live and to "follow your bliss" as Joseph Campbell put it. The dictionary definition of the verb "to inspire" is both to inhale and to "fill someone with the urge or ability to do or feel something, especially to do something creative." The act of breathing (living) is the ultimate creative, inspired act. If we are experiencing grief, fear, heartbreak, overwhelm, and a lack of unconditional love, our

Breath is life ...

inspiration to live and our ability to breathe may be adversely affected. It's as if we literally cannot take life in, which shows up as blockages in the airways, congestion, shortness of breath. On the other hand, if we are feeling great and catch a chest cold or worse, the inability to receive enough oxygen can certainly have a dour effect on our mental/emotional experience since struggling for air is exhausting and frightening.

I had an experience during the writing of my first book that, for me, forever confirmed, beyond any trace of doubt, the mind-body connection. My mother was diagnosed with stage 4 lung cancer and my life took a sharp, dramatic turn. After a few months of living the mantra "I am overwhelmed" attempting to be everything to everyone while managing my own feelings of terror and shock, I found myself extremely ill, unable to breathe or move. When the urgent-care doctor told me I had severe bacterial pneumonia, I was amazed, but not surprised, to hear that it was in the exact same location as my mother's tumor. Once I was on the path to healing, I found this exhilarating and beautiful.

Our body wisdom is beyond the scope of what we can usually imagine, and yet so perfectly tuned in. If we can learn the language of this mind-body connection and communicate with ourselves daily with love and attention, our lives become inspired in every moment. My mother's illness, her healing path, and my experience opened up a new level of awareness.

... the lungs are where breath lives

as long as we live

When the breath is taken away and given back, it's like the gift of life returned in 3D Technicolor. Visualize that your lungs are filled with branches and leaves extending from your sternum. They glow and quiver as the breeze of your breath cleanses and nourishes. This practice purifies, relaxes, and rejuvenates the lungs.

BREATH AWARENESS OR UJJAYI BREATH

If you are very congested and have difficulty breathing, practice Breath Awareness (page 17). If not, practice *Ujjayi* (page 18). Take up the mudra opposite and do a minimum of 10 breaths. Continue for as long as you are inspired.

BE THE VICTOR, NOT THE VICTIM, WITH UJJAYI BREATH

I like to think of the heart as the CEO and visionary of my company, which is my whole being. My mind is the high-level executive assistant, who is organized, sharp, and can get things done. But if my mind is too busy and overworked, or takes over the role of the heart as chief, the company suffers greatly, lacking meaning and purpose, and drowning in messy, unimportant details. No one wants to fall victim to the turbulence of their own mind and lose sight of the grand picture and purpose of life, which is to be, do, and act from love. Ujjayi Breath *keeps the mind focused and quiet and allows the heart to be heard without having to raise her voice.*

MUKULA MUDRA
(Bird Beak Mudra)

- Bring the fingertips of each hand together to touch.
- Place them each 2 inches (5cm) under the center of your right and left collarbones respectively.
- Press firmly, but not hard, and visualize white light pouring into and throughout your chest.

joint pain **oil the hinges**

When I think of joint pain, I think of the Tin Man in *The Wizard of Oz*. He was stiff, stuck, and lonely until he made friends and went on a quest for a heart. The meaningful friendships he made thawed him from his vulnerable and frozen state.

While there are numerous reasons for joint pain (also called arthralgia) including damage, disease, injury, bursitis, osteoarthritis, rheumatoid arthritis, surgery, and inflammation in the joints, one cause isn't often discussed—stress inflammation. A gentle yoga practice can work wonders regardless of the diagnostic cause of the joint pain, but a special treasure trove of relief can be found by specifically addressing stress-related inflammation in the joints. Stress has many triggers, but the kind that can become quite insidious, and often produces inflammation, is the low grade, chronic release of cortisol. Big traumatic events are not to blame for the relentless trickle of stress hormones into the system, but daily overwhelm, loneliness, isolation, or lack of community may be.

Chronic pain is another cause, and the subsequent shifts in your lifestyle to manage it. If you have lost mobility due to joint pain, you may feel the emotional wrench of no longer being able to take part in activities that brought you joy and the kinship of those with whom you shared your passions. This kind of stress can cause or increase inflammation as the body tries to defend itself. To add fuel to the fire, less movement increases stiffness in the joints and aggravates inflammation in many cases. It may feel as if you are

Unity brings fluidity, grace and ease ...

alone in the forest, unable to scratch your own back. I imagine the Tin Man felt rather forsaken and hopeless when he couldn't even lift his own arm to oil his joints. If only he had known the power of the breath to relax him a little. But then, along came some warm-hearted friends and his heart began to glow as their love opened the floodgates. Soon he was awash in the warm fuzzy effects of oxytocin—the happy love hormone! By expressing loving kindness toward yourself through a mindful practice of breath and mudras, you can begin your own happy-ending story.

This practice will stimulate your nadis (energy channels), which will lubricate your joints, increase your flexibility, and soothe your nervous system. A cooling breath relieves some of the hot pain of inflammation and intense emotions, and a warming mudra softens stiff joints. Don't always practice alone. Share the magic by inviting friends or family to join you. The breath and mudras are suitable for everyone and sometimes, as the old adage advocates, the more the merrier.

COOLING OR HISSING BREATH

Take up a comfortable, seated position (page 15), and practice 1–3 rounds of Cooling or Hissing Breath (page 24). Then, if you choose, add the mudras on the following page, a different one for each hand. This creates a balance in the system that is especially effective for joint pain. Once you have the mudras in place, practice between 10 and 30 rounds of breath. If needed, rest at 10-round intervals.

... *find a kind heart to warm you*

SHUNI MUDRA *(Seal of Patience)*

- On the left hand touch the tip of the thumb to the tip of the middle finger.
- Extend the other fingers.
- Place your hand, palm up, on your left thigh.

SURYA RAVI MUDRA *(Sun Mudra)*

This is very similar to *Prithvi Mudra* (sometimes also called *Surya Mudra*), but here the tips of the fingers touch.

- On the right hand touch the tip of the thumb to the tip of the ring finger.
- Extend the other fingers.
- Place your hand, palm up, on your right thigh.

I am fluid and flexible. I am unity and harmony.

JEWEL THOUGHT

carpal tunnel carpe diem!

Oddly, my first experience with Carpal Tunnel Syndrome came from a yoga job. To be exact, it was my first desk job, which was at a yoga studio. After hours of signing students into classes I developed the telltale signs of a throbbing nervy ache in my inner wrist that wrapped around my forearm and elbow. It was a painful inconvenience that severely impacted my life. If this section applies to you, you know how difficult it is to enjoy work or life when your hands are rendered useless. Even opening a jar became a heroic feat during this dark passage. I ended up wearing a cumbersome wrist brace and engaged in constant efforts to execute a more ergonomic, yet feng-shui compliant, office design. A lot of ice was also involved, but fortunately no surgery followed.

Truly the destiny of this happening in a yoga studio was divine. For the first time, I began to practice with the focus on healing a specific physical ailment—and it worked! Good news, as the statistics are dire from the National Institute for Occupational Safety and Health. They cite that carpal tunnel surgery is the second most common type of surgery in the US today. Similarly, a study in the BMJ showed that the prevalence and indicence of carpal tunnel syndrome had increased between 1993 and 2013.

It takes 8 ounces (220g) of force to depress one computer key, so working at a computer all day, five days a week, produces a hefty amount of pressure on your fingers and wrists, and this doesn't include the use of phones, iPads, or other tech gadgets. The painful symptoms come from inflammation of the median nerve. Beside excess pressure on the wrists, other causes are poor circulation and obstructed blood flow, which, if not properly treated, can lead to atrophy in the hands.

In addition to taking stretch breaks and attending to posture and ergonomics, a mudra practice will improve the circulation, flexibility, and strength of your hands. Related conditions, such as tendonitis, osteoarthritis, and tennis and golf elbow, can be helped by this practice as well. Whenever I feel a twinge, I devote some extra time to my hand yoga practice and the combination of that and a bit of ice leaves me with a cool head and pain-free hands, ready to seize the day!

UJJAYI BREATH

To encourage proper circulation and release muscular tension, spend a few minutes with *Ujjayi Breath* (page 18) and then add in the mudra below. Continue for 10–30 rounds.

HAKINI MUDRA *(Power or Rule Mudra)* WITH VARIATIONS

This moving mudra is a variation on the version where the fingertips remain still and touching (see page 125). It may take a little time to get used to but it's worth it! Don't forget to do warm-up exercises for your hands (page 32), which are especially beneficial here. Use firm but gentle pressure to keep the fingers and knuckles touching throughout the practice, and make sure your hands remain level with the elbows.

THE WORLD IS AT YOUR FINGERTIPS

Hakini Mudra *is a favorite mudra of mine in every one of its variations, because all of the fingertips get to meet each other. It awakens relationships in the nerve endings of the fingers, which can awaken new insights and forge new channels of awareness.* Hakini *works like a genie to magically pull us into the moment and to amp up our powers to manifest brilliance quickly.*

- In front of your chest, touch the fingertips of one hand to the fingertips of the other, elbows bent and hands level with them.
- Fold your index fingers into your palms with knuckles touching and hold them with your thumbs.
- Take 3 *Ujjayi Breaths*.
- Stretch the index fingers out, tips touching again and fold in the middle fingers, knuckles touching, and hold them with your thumbs.
- Take 3 *Ujjayi Breaths*.
- Continue with the ring and pinky fingers, and then reverse the process from pinky to index fingers.
- Do 3 rounds total and then rest your hands while breathing naturally.

back pain repair and rejoice

Back pain is quite simply a pain in the…let's just say back. It's of epidemic proportions to the point that, when asked at the beginning of a yoga class if there are any injuries of concern, people offer it up casually, as though it's a given. The reply comes with a dismissive wave, a mumbled "just back pain," and is often punctuated with a resigned, sheepish shrug. This is for the chronically affected. Then there's the hobbled victim of back pain who dreams of getting onto a mat or even into a car, but finds themselves prone on the floor, or in bed, at frequent intervals. One statistic from The Lancet states that back pain affects 1 in 10 people worldwide. No wonder it's being treated as an unwelcome but inevitable norm.

A plethora of reasons exist for the affliction, and a bushel of diagnoses reflecting specific types of back trouble, but one thing is for certain—sitting for too long is not pretty. Our lifestyles have evolved (or perhaps devolved) to more time on bottoms than feet. This is often the cause of back pain, as we compress the lower vertebrae and squeeze the "jelly" out of the precious shock absorbers (spinal discs), leaving us literally high and dry. It's like running out of oil and the ride feels like an old jalopy on a dirt road.

Beside a seated lifestyle, causes of early spinal-disc degeneration include poor posture, injury, strain due to excessive exercise, too little exercise, gardening, and aging. No car can withstand the wear and tear of the road over time and no spine can either. But that being said, there is much we can do to support, strengthen, adjust, and care for our backs in a way that prevents injury, prolongs suppleness, and soothes aches.

Even though lower back pain (it even has its own medical acronym—LBP) is second only to the common cold in reasons to visit the doctor, most cases are actually difficult to diagnose. This is because it is often "non-specific" or "musculoskeletal," and here is where we can be really effective in our home yoga practice. That kind of pain is due to muscular tension—contraction of the back muscles—which is often the manifestation of stress and anxiety. Think of your whole body holding its breath tensely when you are under stress or feeling anxious. Now think of that happening many times throughout the day, every day. The back is especially prone to holding this tension without our being aware of it. It is the workhorse of your body, always jumping in to do the work while your core muscles are floating on a raft in the islands. The back also jumps in to tidy up our relationship and work anxieties, absorbing those stressful emotions. By stimulating the reflexology points in the hands corresponding to particular muscles and relaxing the nervous system through the breath, we can give the back a little vacation.

MOON BREATH

This calming breath (page 21) relaxes mind and muscles. Practice between 10 and 30 rounds. Then, if taking the mudra, practice it with Breath Awareness (page 17), cultivating a tranquil mind.

MINDFUL MOON BREATHING

Though it is magnificent to behold, the moon's power is less flashy than the sun. It's cool, calm, and patient. One could say the moon is mindful. Oftentimes when I have suffered from back injury or pain, it's when I have overworked myself, or been in the grips of emotional urgency and made a sudden move to lift or force something. Or I've simply forgotten to stand up and stretch between bouts of sitting. There are many moments in life that we cannot account for, but whether we are focused on preventing pain or healing from it, a few patient moments of calming moon breath can cast a soft light by which to surrender and back off.

BACK MUDRA

Some mudras, including this one, don't translate into Sanskrit. Although each hand takes a different position, Back Mudra is considered to be one therapeutic mudra.

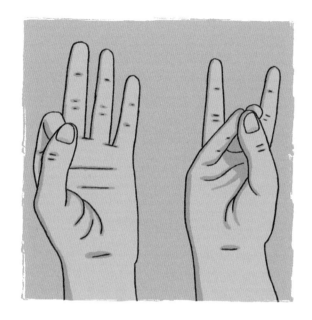

- With the right hand touch the thumb, middle finger, and pinky together.
- With the left hand, place the nail of the index finger into the first joint of the thumb extending the other fingers.
- Place your hands, palms up, on your thighs.
- For guidance on how long to hold the mudra, see Therapeutic Mudras (page 34).

I take life one breath at a time.
I release all tension.

JEWEL THOUGHT

immune system and thyroid function **all systems are up**

The thyroid is a beautiful, butterfly-shaped gland in the base of the throat and, despite its delicate appearance, it is a powerfully important piece of the puzzle that is you. Part of the endocrine system, it produces hormones that regulate breathing, heart rate, metabolism, muscle strength, body temperature, menstrual cycles, mood, brain development, digestion, and bone maintenance.

The immune system has a big part to play in every aspect of health, of course, and is closely connected to the thyroid remaining in balance, neither underactive (hypothyroidism) nor overactive (hyperthyroidism). So the thyroid is the perfect place to begin to chart a course of healing. A weak immune system cannot do its detective work to expose the pathogens (disease-causing agents) hiding among the healthy tissues of the body, which affects the functioning of the thyroid and may cause the imbalance that we notice as symptoms. The seed of the imbalance may be planted in the malfunctioning of the immune system, and correcting and improving that will make any thyroid treatment more effective.

With autoimmune disorders we have a confused system that is fighting against its own army. The way we can work with our breath and mudra practice to address this is to restore some clarity and harmony to our central nervous system (CNS) and to soothe the adrenal glands. The CNS and adrenal glands are strongly influenced by the thyroid and the immune system, and are very susceptible to stress. We start once again with the focus on creating a more harmonious environment and keeping our stress responses in check. This is why the practice of yoga can make a vital and pivotal contribution to your healing path.

The thyroid is located in the region of the throat chakra (*vishuddha*) and a breath and mudra practice that nourishes this energy center can also enhance communication, the ability to listen and express your truth.

BEE BREATH

This breath is wonderful for your mood as it balances levels of serotonin, "the happy hormone," in your brain. Once you are in a comfortable seated or standing position (page 15), start the breathing practice (page 25). If using the mudra, add it after one breath. Continue with Bee Breath for 5–10 rounds, taking a little break in between rounds to feel the vibration. You can add a visual of a turquoise butterfly right in the center of your throat, if it appeals to you. Turquoise is the color of the throat chakra.

GRANTHITA MUDRA *(The Knot)*

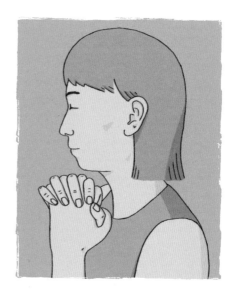

- Interlace your fingers so that the left thumb is on top.
- The tips of the thumbs touch the tips of the index fingers on both hands.
- Hold the mudra in front of your throat but not touching.

My entire being expresses harmony and health.

JEWEL THOUGHT

fatigue reboot and be reborn

The dictionary dishes up these two definitions for fatigue, side by side:

1 Extreme tiredness, typically resulting from mental or physical exertion or illness.
2 A group of soldiers ordered to perform menial, nonmilitary tasks, sometimes as punishment.

Now it stands to reason that we become exhausted when we are under duress, overworked, have fallen ill, encounter major life changes, hormonal fluctuations, or insomnia, experience mental disturbances, have poor nutrition, lack exercise, and so on.

The second definition is the one that caught my eye. I'm aware of the term "fatigue" for a group of soldiers, but it was news to me that this group was enlisted to perform menial tasks that held no relevance to their network, and as a sort of punishment. A light bulb flickered in my mind as I thought of the statistic that 1 in 3 Americans report feeling fatigued on a regular basis and that one study cited in the Huffington Post reported that 76% of the 1,139 employees taking part felt tired on many days of the week—15% of these people fall asleep at work at least once a week! Now couple these findings with the mysterious and cure-resistant Chronic Fatigue Syndrome storm that has raged for decades—according to an article in *Metro*, chronic fatigue syndrome (CFS/ME) affects around 250,000 people in the UK with varying levels of severity; some people are just managing to function while others are completely bed-ridden. It's a very curious mix. Beside all the usual thieves that rob us of energy as mentioned above, there could be a widespread soul system meltdown. If your work/life is lacking luster, you feel estranged in your community, or your relationships are stale, this can drain your life force.

In yoga and ayurveda (the sister science and whole-health system from India) the whole person and all aspects of life are examined when there is imbalance. Under this paradigm, if we are soldiering on feeling a lack of purpose and meaningful connections, our entire internal eco-system can be thrown off. Humans are pack animals and as such need a place in the order of things that matter. If we don't have that, we may grow uninspired and very tired. Tedium can be torturous.

Whatever the root cause of your fatigue, it's always a good idea to take a wide-angle approach. In addition to the basics of food, sleep, and exercise, what interests and excites you? Is there call for a new experience or hobby? Is there room for growth in your work? Are you engaged in community? The eternal now is a perfect moment to assess, reboot, and perhaps rebirth some aspect of your life. You can make a tiny shift in habits or you can go massive. Whether you're short on sleep or soul searching, a perfect start is to incorporate this sunny mood-enhancing and energy-boosting practice.

SUN BREATH

There's nothing like the energy of the sun to make you feel alive. This breath (page 20) is like a shot of sunshine for your soul. Practice a few rounds, then add the mudra opposite with your free hand and continue for 5–10 rounds minimum.

With every breath I feel my mind, body, and soul reawaken. I am alive with possibility.

JEWEL THOUGHT

PRITHVI MUDRA *("The Vast One"/Earth Mudra)*

This mudra increases vitality, strength, and endurance and is said to counter vitamin deficiencies, nourishing hair, bones, and blood. It balances earth and fire elements for a grounded energy boost. Use your right hand for Sun Breath and your left hand for the mudra.

- Either place your left hand on your thigh with palm facing up or bend your arm at the elbow and hold your hand at shoulder height. Hand on thigh is a bit more grounding and hand up is more energizing.
- Fold the ring finger into the palm and hold it down with the thumb.
- Extend index, middle, and pinky fingers upward.

fertility **prepare the soil**

A vibrant, fragrant fruit grows from nutrient-rich soil. Anything we seek to bring to fruition, be it a human life, a painting, a delicious meal, or a bountiful garden, requires a subtle blend of effort and patience. It also requires respect for mystery and quiet contemplation. We can read the books, gather the paintbrushes, stock the ingredients, and test the conditions, but it is often our surrender to divine mother nature that produces the freedom from which creation flows. While there is perfect natural order in our world, it is not often up to us in which way this order unfolds.

I woke up one day on the cusp of the abyss and, like the famous Roy Lichtenstein painting, I gasped, "I forgot to have a child!" I had been busy with a full (often chaotic), creative life and somehow time slipped away. Then it hit me hard—I wanted to create a child! Or at least be a vessel for this new spark of divinity to make her home. The statistics were not in my favor, nor were my husbands, but the desire defied them and we set sail for this land. The journey was not without its stormy passages, but when all was said and done, I learned a kind of surrender as we stood in a river in Costa Rica and prayed to the water gods that it was meant to be. And it (or rather SHE) was!

There was more to it, of course, but beside the obvious steps, the biggest for me was letting go. Oh no, not again with the letting go! Yes. Our job is to heed the call to create, prepare a loving environment, and then relax into the blissful vibration that drew us into this fertile valley to begin with. All creations

Creative life force is longing to be revealed through you...

...relax and let it flow

are less about following instructions and getting it right than about relaxing into the sacredness of being part of the mystery of it all. If we can surrender the urge to micromanage ourselves out of the joy and trust our inner guidance system, a whole universe of support will surround us, as if we are in a safe and sacred womb. Cultivating the intoxication of the original impulse to produce (or reproduce!) releases all sorts of delicious chemicals that are needed to bring the seed to life. When we slow down, tune in, and stay connected, we are bathed in the happy juices of serotonin, oxytocin, dopamine, and endorphins. Connecting with ourselves, our mate, and the magic of life builds trust and patience (handy for parents and all creators) and is the nutrient-rich soil that is often forgotten in our busy worlds, as we add "have a baby" or "write a book" to the list. Time spent preparing the soil is an opportunity to relish one season of your life as you look forward to another.

THREE-PART BREATH

Three-part Breath (page 19) is grounding, calming, and perfect for relieving the anxiety and urgency that can creep in and constrict the life force. Practice 10–30 rounds. Then, if using the mudra, release the breath and follow the instructions overleaf.

All that is sacred grows in me. I'm a shining vessel of love and light.

JEWEL THOUGHT

YONI MUDRA *(Uterus or Origin Mudra)*

There are variations on this mudra and I am choosing this one for its elegance, simplicity, and effectiveness. It improves the health of the sexual organs for men and women, invites in the divine feminine, makes the sacred connection, and can boost fertility.

- Press your thumbs together pointing up at your navel.
- Press your index fingers together pointing out in front of you.
- Fold the rest of your fingers into your palms with the knuckles touching.
- As you inhale, keep the thumbs in your navel and point your index fingers up toward your ribs letting your belly expand and pelvis tilt forward toward the ground.
- As you exhale, keep the thumbs in your navel, let your index fingers drop to point down toward your pelvis, and contract your abdomen so that your pelvis tilts up toward you.
- Find a rhythm and gently rock in and out of the breath, expanding and contracting with each breath and keeping your thumbs anchored in your navel.
- Practice for 3 minutes or 30 rounds. This mudra is especially pleasurable with soft music, especially chanting or music designed for the sacral chakra. This is the energy center for pleasure, so the more you can allow yourself to experience it, the more your creativity and fertility will flow!

sexual life force
harness the power of creation

Sexual health and the awakening of the sexual life force is an important aspect of the ayurvedic view of health and well-being. This view contends that everything is connected and we can't reach our maximum potential without nurturing the whole being. This is apparent even in the meaning of the word yoga—union, be that union with our own true nature, union with the divine, or union with another.

We will take a peek at tantra yoga (a form of hatha yoga), which is often thought of as the yoga of sex, but actually means to weave or expand. It's the threading together of *asanas*, mudras, mantras, the *bandhas* (energy locks), and the chakras in order to expand consciousness and experience bliss. Sexuality is an important component of this spiritual practice and must be included in order to create a truly balanced and dynamic state of being. Our sexual organs affect our moods and energy levels, our creativity and motivation. A yoga practice involving breath and mudra is one way to keep the organs in the second chakra (*swadhisthana*, the sexual center) healthy. Of course, there are other wonderful ways, such as sex itself, but it's important to note that our relationship to our sexuality will shift and change at different stages of life. A healthy sex life boosts your immune system, releases endorphins, and relieves stress. Sexual desire and the urge to enjoy a healthy, safe sex life is very much a beautiful and joyful part of the human experience.

However, it is not necessary to force desire in a time of voluntary abstinence in order to be healthy. The mudra and breath in this practice can keep the second chakra glowing. When we stay in tune with our highest self and seek presence and authenticity of being, we can cultivate health and balance naturally. The more mindful and awake we become through the practice, the more we hear the body speak and notice if the body needs a sexual release. In addition to feeling good, sexual release is a natural cleanser, eliminating bacteria and fungi for women and blocked prana for both men and women.

The sexual life force can be awakened for the purpose of divine spiritual connection, physical intimacy and love, and even creative pursuits.

It is important to mention that although our bodies do change and our sex lives may follow, advancing in age is not necessarily the end! In addition to the possibility of prolonging sexual vitality, a regular practice can lead to a more graceful relationship with our bodies, at any age. The key to bringing a yogic perspective into the proverbial bedroom is to cultivate sensitivity, awareness, and acceptance as you weave together your unique tapestry of joy and bliss.

SKULL SHINING BREATH WITH ROOT LOCK
(Mula Bandha)

Once you are in a comfortable, seated position (page 15), practice one round of Skull Shining Breath (page 23). Then add the mudra, if using, and the root lock. The root lock takes time to refine, but even for beginners it will tone the pelvic floor and sex organs, and is both invigorating and calming. When you complete the last exhale of the Skull Shining Breath, contract the perineal muscles in the pelvic floor from anus to genitals and hold with an inhale for 10–15 seconds. Practice between 5 and 10 rounds with breath, mudra (if using), and root lock.

This practice is not recommended during pregnancy or for those with hypertension or panic disorder. Instead, practice Ujjayi Breath (page 18) for 1–3 minutes.

KUNDALINI MUDRA

There isn't a short English translation for this mudra. *Kundalini* is the latent female (*shakti*) energy coiled at the base of the spine. When activated, it travels up the spine until we reach our full and balanced potential.

This mudra unites the masculine and feminine energies to awaken and activate sexual life force.

- Wrap your right hand around your left index finger.
- Both hands are fists.
- Elbows are bent and the closed palms are facing you.

I am alive with the power of all creation.

JEWEL THOUGHT

weight loss
thank you and goodbye

There are many reasons why we may be carrying some extra weight and we owe it to ourselves to take a closer look. Whether you simply feel heavier than you'd prefer, or risk heart disease from being overweight, your mental and physical health are at stake.

The reasons for carrying excess weight may be genetic, or due to various medical disorders, limited access to the outdoors or healthy food choices, lack of nutrition education or support, boredom, or deep-rooted emotional trauma. In addition to addressing the medical aspects with the proper healthcare professionals, we serve ourselves well if we sit down and have a heart to heart with the weight. It has a voice and may enjoy being heard.

The underlying root causes, if you can identify them and anything else that aggravates the situation, can provide important clues or entire missing pieces. Some quiet, mindful moments to hear the sound of your soul may reveal some very poignant information. Perhaps you are simply too busy and exhausted to sort out a plan and you need guidance and some schedule changes. Maybe you haven't allowed yourself to process some important pieces of your life experience and could benefit from the ear of a therapist. It could be that change is your bugaboo. Whatever you hear, it's time to explore self-love as the best thing you could do for your health. A good open conversation in the spirit of self-acceptance and compassion can be the beginning of healthy change. Listen with loving kindness, and thank your beautiful body for bringing this to your attention.

Remind yourself frequently as you connect to yourself and your body that you are, and always have been, enough. Ultimately, it doesn't matter what you wear and what size it is as long as you are comfortable with yourself, in good health and at ease. If you are ready to let go of a few—or a lot of—pounds, try saying, "Thank you for all you have meant to me and taught me. Thank you for being there for me. Thank you, and goodbye!"

SKULL SHINING BREATH

This purifying, energizing breath works the abdominals, aids digestion, and boosts metabolism. Sit comfortably (page 15) and begin (page 23). If you are using the mudra, take 10 warm-up breaths first. Practice for 3–5 rounds.

This practice is not recommended during pregnancy or for those with hypertension or panic disorder. Instead, practice *Ujjayi Breath* (page 18) for 1–3 minutes.

PRITHVI MUDRA *(Earth Mudra)*

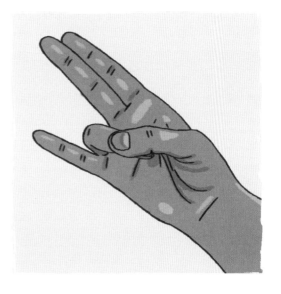

This mudra has a few variations and is also commonly called the Sun Mudra since it invokes *agni* (fire energy) while balancing earth energy, which works with digestion, metabolism, and is said to control hunger.

- Place your hands, palms up, on your thighs, or hold up your hands with bent elbows at shoulder height.
- Bend your ring fingers on each hand into your palm.
- Press the thumbs into the ring fingers, holding them down.
- The index and middle fingers extend, touching each other.
- The pinky fingers extend.

I am whole and complete. I am filled with light and love.

JEWEL THOUGHT

CHAPTER 4
BREATHING AND MUDRAS FOR THE SOUL

In this chapter, we explore how breathing and mudras can help matters of the mind, heart, and soul. They are just as important as physical conditions—as we saw in Chapter 3, these emotional and mental issues are sometimes a root cause of what is ailing us physically.

addiction relax, you are enough!

There are as many forms of addiction as there are reasons we become addicts. One common root cause for this itchy, restless desire to do, change, or escape something is that, somehow, we are not enough, or our life as it is falls short. Addiction is considered a primary chronic disease that is based on the brain's need for reward.

Addictive behavior ranges from routinely partaking in the subtle and satisfying morning coffee ritual to the relentless pursuit of soul-crushing, life-ruining obsessions that tear families and lives apart. We can even develop addictions to unhealthy thought patterns that form new neural pathways in the brain, reinforcing the negative pattern and behavior. When in the grip of a loop or an impulse, we may feel besieged from all directions. The body struggles to balance its hormones, the mind struggles to focus, and the emotional undercurrents of fear, guilt, anger, regret, and shame rage below the surface. A regular day can feel like a minefield of triggers while dodging grenades. We may avoid situations by staying home only to find that the TV remote, computers, and smartphones are rarely far from our fingertips, and those devices deliver a steady stream of distraction and desire, suggesting that we are always just one click away from satisfaction. Overuse of these devices is addictive in itself!

The good news is that the challenge of addiction can be a portal to discovering the highest version of yourself. It can lead to new levels of awareness and compassion. We have the power to rewire our brains and form healthier neural pathways by replacing bad habits with good ones. We can shift from the drama of extremes to the sanctity of balance.

Where you are is exactly where you need to be ...

For some guidance, we can focus on the yogic concepts of *raga*—attachment, that which we crave—and *dvesha*—aversion, that which we seek to avoid. Wherever the attachments and avoidances are coming from, if we can add some presence, acceptance, and trust in ourselves, we can gain insight, clarity, and space between the thoughts. *Raga* and *dvesha* are two contrasting ends of experience and the sweet spot is in the middle. We can disrupt our tendencies toward the extremes by dropping into the moment and observing the impulse without acting on it. According to the teachings of Abraham and Esther Hicks (see Resources, page 141), if we can sustain that disruption for 17 seconds and build from there, we can begin to rewire the system. The breath and mudras are especially useful here, since addictions are often rituals that involve our hands and the overflow of thoughts. By engaging your hands with a mudra and your mind with your breath, you can ease your way into the present and possibly find exactly what you have been looking for right in your own heart.

EQUAL BREATH

This breath can be practiced seated, standing, or lying down (page 15). It's described on page 18. Begin the breath and the mudra together. If you are feeling especially agitated, after a few rounds pause for a count of 4 after the inhale and a count of 4 after the exhale, so it becomes a "square breath" of 4 counts for each action. Practice breath and mudra (if using) for 10 rounds minimum and build from there. Continue for as long as you need.

... be still, listen, and trust

KALESVARA MUDRA

This mudra is dedicated to the goddess Kalesvara, who rules over time. We invoke her to reconnect to the present moment, clearing our attachments to the past and projections of the future. Spending more time in the NOW can liberate you.

- Hold your hands in front of your chest, palms facing each other.
- Press the pads of your middle fingers into each other.
- Bend the index, ring and pinky fingers, into your palms and press the knuckles into each other.
- Point the thumbs toward your chest.

Everything I need is here in this moment.
I am here.

JEWEL THOUGHT

harmony and balance
nature's way

One of the gifts of time spent in nature is the spectacle of balance and harmony being played out before our eyes. The cycle of life is everywhere from the rise and set of the sun each day to the year-long dance of seasons that trees perform with grace and beauty. We follow this cycle when we rise and are born anew each day, and when we sleep and experience a mini death. We participate in the rhythm of nature as we shine our light outward like the sun fostering growth, and when we retreat, reflect, and travel inward to the cool lunar spaces within. Balancing the energy between activity and stillness is a central component in a mindful, healthful yoga practice. If we can find inspiration and example in nature, that can help us to tune in to our own natural rhythms. The more we slow down and check in, the more we come to hear the language of the body, and we can interpret and use what we hear to make choices that bring balance and peace.

A lovely piece of yogic philosophy, and a beautiful Sanskrit word, speaks of this—*sattva*. It is one of the three *gunas*, or qualities, that comprise everything in existence. *Guna* means "that which binds; strand or fiber." *Sattva* is the quality of light, serenity, balance, peacefulness, equilibrium, and transcendence. It comes between *rajas* (activity, passion, desire, effort, pain) and *tamas* (inertia, procrastination, lethargy, ignorance, attachment). All three of the *gunas* interact and relate to each other throughout our daily existence. Each of them signifies necessary aspects of life and holds a place in the life cycle. The level of these qualities within us tends to vary at different moments and stages of life, but we can keep *sattva* high through practices such as mudras and breath.

In bug life, the animal kingdom, and the entire natural world on land and in the sea, there is an orderly chaos, an epic design that is bound to balance and ensures adherence to a harmony larger than any one individual aspect. Each individual element is its own universe and yet is ultimately woven and threaded into the larger design as is a single thread in a grand tapestry. Humans are no different, which is becoming increasingly apparent as we learn that our actions and intentions affect the earth and each other all across the globe. If we focus on inner harmony, we serve our personal ecosystem, resulting in balance and greater health and happiness. This light and clarity touches others and they carry that light forward and so on. With one balanced thread at a time, we can bring more peace and harmony to the world.

ALTERNATE NOSTRIL BREATH

This clarifying and balancing breath practice (page 22), also called Sun/Moon breath, is excellent for creating a sattvic feeling of light and harmony. Practice 10–30 rounds from a comfortable seated position (page 15). Then release the breath and practice the mudra on its own if you feel inspired to do so.

I feel whole and balanced. I enjoy the rhythm of life.

JEWEL THOUGHT

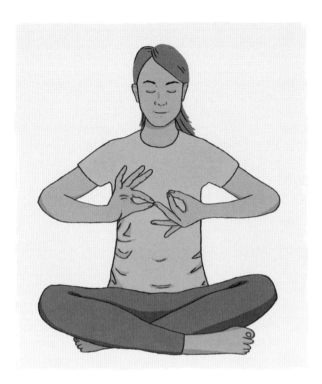

DHARMACHAKRA MUDRA *(The Wheel of Dharma)*

This mudra symbolizes the continuous flow of energies and time cycles, and our connection to inner and outer worlds.

- Bring the thumb and index fingers of each hand to touch.
- With arms raised to the side and elbows bent, position both hands in front of your chest at heart level.
- Face the palm of your left hand toward your body and the palm of the right hand away from your body.
- Touch the middle finger of the left hand to the place where the right index finger and thumb connect. Keep the other fingers extended.
- Close your eyes and breath naturally for 3 minutes. You can count your breaths (which will be approximately 30) or I like to use a sand timer.

trust cruise control

Trust is such a simple, solid, unassuming word yet it is loaded with emotion. Trust is both action and surrender. It is a choice we make to hand over the steering wheel. This can be very challenging for many of us. We may see ourselves as the captain of our own ship and feel, as the captain does, that all of the responsibility lies with us to live a wonderful life. This can be quite isolating and frightening at times. If it is solely up to us to navigate a safe passage and find the destination in a timely manner, while ensuring that all aboard are taken care of and have their needs met, we can feel overwhelmed, or even resentful at times. In this scenario, even with a robust and willing crew, the final decisions inevitably fall into the captain's lap.

We are all captains in various ways—as parents, employees and employers, and with the details of our own inner lives—but it is an illusion to believe that we are in this alone. Life is filled with creative touches, synchronicities, and divine intervention. As quickly as a storm can rise and obscure all hope of a safe landing on solid ground, the sun can burst through and light our way toward an even more beautiful and unexpected experience.

We choose trust a hundred times a day in small and big ways—as we get into our cars, guide our children toward independence, fall in love, take steps toward our dreams—and yet it is easy to be derailed and feel we are going it alone. It takes willpower, courage, and an adventurous spirit to choose to trust when the cards seem stacked against us. Yet it is precisely in that moment that an act of surrender can liberate us and give rise to clarity and direction. A regular practice of handing over some of your "to-do list" to the universe can bring some amazing results. Act on what you know you can do. Hoist the sails, clean the engine, stock supplies, and chart your course. But once you are on the high seas of your life, try, on regular occasions, to sit back, hands off the helm, face to the wind, and enjoy some cruise control. After all, the infinite intelligence that gave you an ocean to sail on certainly can handle the navigation for a few minutes here and there—not to mention that a well-rested and relaxed captain runs a much pleasanter ship.

BEE BREATH

This breath balances serotonin (happy hormone) levels, and fosters a feeling of belonging. Sit, stand, or lie down (page 15) and practice Bee Breath (page 25) for 3 rounds to clear the mind and heart. If you are adding the mudra, do so after the breath and hold it in silence for as long as you like, breathing naturally.

VAJRAPRADAMA MUDRA *(Thunderbolt Mudra)*

Like the word trust, this mudra is simple but powerful. *Vajra* means both thunderbolt and diamond, which suggests something unbreakable and unstoppable. It is known as the mudra for unshakeable trust and helps to secure our relationship to divine guidance.

- Interlace your fingers, keeping palms open.
- Place your hands on your chest at heart center.
- Hold as long as you like, feeling the presence of your being in the rise and fall of your chest.

The universe loves, supports, and guides me. We are more powerful together.

JEWEL THOUGHT

courage **a matter of the heart**

Like the voice of the heart, courage can be a whisper or a roar. It can be manipulated, conjured, and sometimes even dragged out of us. It can also come quietly in the morning as our feet touch the cold floor and we hope for the best. I have lived both types of courage many times over, and I have seen that, like the heart, it is both a muscle that can be strengthened and an organ with a purpose. The purpose of courage, as I see it, is to make friends with fear. Franklin D. Roosevelt said, "The only thing we have to fear is fear itself," but I know that when I ignore my fears it's like fear fertilizer. Fear gives us an opportunity to explore more of who we are, and, as a bonus, fear can truly keep us safe as when you bolt from danger or take a mindful detour. Fear itself is not to be feared but to be heard, rather than blindly obeyed.

FDR went on to identify "nameless, unreasoning, unjustified terror which paralyzes needed efforts to convert retreat into advance." Here is where courage meets fear and befriends it—when you feel that tickle down your back, somersault in your belly, or cold rush in your heart center and you send courage to greet it and say, "Hello, what's on your mind, Fear? What do I need to know or do here?" Although action may be warranted, on many occasions we discover there is nothing to do but rather a feeling to sit with, courageously. We might just need to take the cold hand of fear into the warm hand of courage and wait. As we wait, we grow stronger, and the heart does its exquisite work of pumping blood and courage through our veins until the next step appears. It's then that courage really takes over with a whisper or a roar.

For courage, we will bravely approach *Abhaya Hrdaya Mudra* with Bellows Breath. The combination of this metabolism boosting breath and this heart strengthening mudra will help to burn away self-doubt and reveal your inner strength. Proceed with ease and a calm mind and you will find yourself radiantly empowered by the light of your heart in no time!

BELLOWS BREATH

Think of a fireplace bellows; this breath will whisk away the ashy build-up of fearful thoughts that cover your brilliance and will illuminate your path. Settle into your seated position (page 15). Practice a round or two of Bellows Breath (page 23) and then take up the mudra below. Once you have the mudra in place begin the breath again for 3 rounds. Between rounds breathe mindfully into the heart center for 3–5 breaths. Incorporate the jewel thought between rounds, or upon completion of the breath, while holding the mudra. This practice is not recommended during pregnancy or for those with hypertension or panic disorder. Instead, follow instructions for *Ujjayi Breath* for 1–3 minutes.

FINDING YOUR COURAGE

Like the Cowardly Lion in The Wizard of Oz, *we can't know who we are or what we are capable of until the opportunity arises and we are tested or confronted regarding something that is close to our hearts. A person, a cause, an injustice, or your heart's vision may inspire a fire within you to protect, honor, change, or preserve something that leads to taking a stand. It is in this moment, no matter how hot it might get, that you feel your courage as power and you know that home is always where your heart is and there's no place like it.*

ABHAYA HRDAYA MUDRA *(Fearless Heart Mudra)*

- Bring your hands in front of your chest, palms facing each other.
- Cross the right wrist over the left with the right hand closest to you, so your palms are now facing outward.
- Hook your right index finger around your left index finger.
- Hook your right middle finger around your left middle finger.
- Hook your right pinky finger around your left pinky finger.
- Touch your thumbs to the tips of your ring fingers.

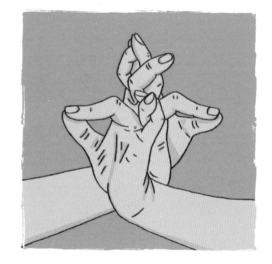

An alternative courage mudra for children or those who find *Abhaya Hrdaya* difficult is *Abhaya Mudra* (Fearless Mudra).

Abhaya Mudra *(Fearless Mudra)*

- Raise your right arm to shoulder height and bend at the elbow.
- Your palm will face forward.
- Place your left hand on your thigh facing up.

I am here. I am safe. The light of my heart will reveal my next step in perfect timing.

JEWEL THOUGHT

confidence there is only one you

It is clear that self-confidence can take you places. Those who seem to own the room or are willing to take risks often seem to get the prize and reap the rewards. But what of those who are the shy, beautiful wallflowers, bringing quiet color to the room? Are they destined to be background music, waiting for the leftovers from their more socially adept peers? According to a popular verse from the Bible—"the meek shall inherit the earth"—it doesn't seem like it.

The meaning of the word "meek" in this context has been the subject of a lot of discourse, and one conclusion is that there is immense power in each of us and how it is demonstrated can vary. A path guided from deep wisdom, connection to source, and humility may not be flashy but those who follow it can have tremendous staying power. You see this story played out in countless coming of age films where the "popular" kids (the most confident) rule the roost during high school, but then cut to their adult life and the tables have turned. What these allegories point to is that we can all benefit from taking a deeper look within ourselves.

Confidence that comes from mastering a skill, achieving a goal, or "getting the girl or boy" is fun and rewarding, but confidence that is built solely on the foundation of what we can DO in the world, rather than who we ARE, wears down as we try to keep up. It may be that we are naturally outgoing and feel at ease at a party, but if that same ease is not present when we are alone with ourselves, the confidence is surface-level and may not last or provide the inner peace we seek and deserve. A lack of true, deep confidence can show up in needing to validate our existence through overachievement. We see this in some highly "successful" people who still feel empty and unfulfilled despite numerous achievements. Conversely someone with a simple life and very little on paper can feel utterly content. It's about self-worth.

From the perspective of wisdom traditions, there is only one you and we are all here on purpose, with purpose. When we learn that being our true selves is all that is needed, we can shine wherever we stand—in the center of the room or the corner. We can achieve mastery from inspiration rather than fear. After all, contrast and diversity are the spice of life and your particular flavor and style add just the right touch to the universe.

Use this mudra and breath to tap into a deeper awareness that you come from the source, you are powerful beyond measure, and you are utterly unique. Just like everyone.

SKULL SHINING OR BELLOWS BREATH

Both of these breaths (page 23) will activate your solar plexus chakra, the center for personal power, authenticity, and confidence. Choose which one appeals to you, practice 2 rounds from a seated position (page 15). Then add the mudra, if using, for another 5–10 rounds.

THE GIFT OF LIGHT

Gemstones are often used for healing as they reflect various qualities that exist within us. Each gemstone has a unique expression, essence, and benefit to the one who holds it. While more people may value a diamond more than obsidian or labradorite, it doesn't mean that only the diamond is worthy of our attention. People are the same way. Some shine more brightly at first glance, but all have the gift of light to offer. The breath and mudra practices can unlock this light, increasing our sense of worth and helping us to better understand our own kind of magnificence.

> I shine with the light of the universe. I am whole and perfect in this moment.
>
> **JEWEL THOUGHT**

Neither of these practices are recommended during pregnancy or for those with hypertension or panic disorder. Instead, practice Equal Breath (page 18), which is excellent for calming and acceptance and can lead to greater confidence as well.

AHAMKARA MUDRA *("I Maker" Mudra)*

This refers to the self as individual and the part of the ego that asserts itself. In people who are timid this mudra can strengthen the "muscle" of the self. It's also wonderful for children who suffer from lack of confidence.

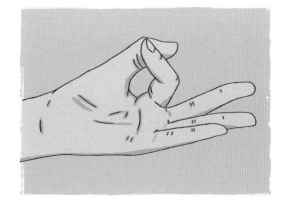

- Press the thumb to the outer edge of first joint of the index finger on each hand.
- The middle, ring, and pinky fingers are extended.
- Place your hands, palms up, on your thighs.

For children, this should be done with Equal Breath (page 18) or natural breathing.

inspiration and creativity
color your life

If your life has fallen into the gray zone, you may be hungry to shake things up a bit. This can happen when routine, responsibility, and life chores have stacked up and suffocated your inner artist. My work is creative by nature, and I also love to create for pleasure, which makes life wonderful when I am brimming with ideas, vision, and inspiration, but disastrous if the river of creativity has run dry! Over time I have discovered that inspiration is everywhere, creativity is in every thing, and manifestation is a matter of focus.

My daughter has a wonderful traveling art kit with a lightweight easel, brushes, paint, and tools. If she has it with her and she's inspired, she can paint! I have created a kit for myself. My body is the case and in it I have my senses: sight, hearing, touch, taste, and smell. When I am feeling stuck, gray, or running dry, I have the most luck getting in the flow when I stop trying so hard and drop into receiving mode. Then I can open the secret compartment in my kit, my sixth sense, and focus on presence.

The sixth sense can be described as our ability to perceive what cannot be seen. It's the subtle dimension or energy body within you and around you, connected to the sixth chakra, or third eye. When we hold focus through meditation, become present to the world around us, and commune with the higher self, we build a bridge between the inner and outer worlds. This bridge is like a speedway to effortless creativity. Holding focus is not always about chaining oneself to the task, but about sustaining a state of presence and mindfulness that allows the river to flow to you, rather than you chasing it. This may be why so many ideas occur to people as they shower, walk, or after a yoga class!

Try my favorite simple trick to stir up some fresh ideas by taking a few minutes outside simply to gaze. This can be done out of a window as well. Then practice the following breath and mudra and get ready for the gift of creativity to land in your open hands and heart.

THREE-PART BREATH

This breath (page 19) is grounding, relaxing, and perfect for opening yourself to inspiration. Sit comfortably (page 15). If you want to add the mudra, you can begin the mudra and breath at the same time, and breathe 5–10 rounds. Then release the breath and if you've taken the mudra, continue to sit quietly with it. Focus your attention on the third eye, the space between the eyebrows, for greater focus if you like.

SWADHISTHANA MUDRA *(One's Own Abode)*

This mudra connects us to the sacral chakra (creative/sexual center) and the element of water, which generates creative flow. It harnesses the sexual life force and sends it up to higher chakras to use imaginatively.

- Place your left hand in your lap palm up.
- Place your right hand, palm up, on top of your left.
- Touch the tips of the thumbs together.

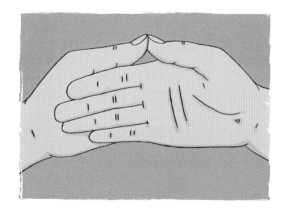

I am open to the creative life force flowing within me, and all around me.

JEWEL THOUGHT

gratitude always the right choice

Gratitude is a self-fulfilling prophecy. The more grateful we are the more there is to be grateful for. Numerous scientific studies have produced fascinating findings about the power of gratitude. For one thing, the more we practice getting into a state of authentic gratitude, the better we feel and therefore the more receptive we are to the beautiful and miraculous moments in our lives, which then seem to multiply right before our eyes! What's more, the studies are finding that the positive effects of gratitude practices are lasting, and can even promote the creation of new, healthy, neural pathways in our brains. This means that, with practice, we can replace toxic, negative thinking habits with optimism, enthusiasm, and joyful thinking! Now that's something to be grateful for!

A feeling of gratitude is often physically felt as warmth and expansion in the heart center. This area of the body is the heart chakra and is home to the thymus gland and the center of the immune system. Although the thymus gland itself has done the heavy lifting of setting up our immune system by puberty, we still have the ability to improve or overtax it throughout our lives. Feeling grateful lends itself to happiness, and the research is pointing to a secure connection between positive emotions and our ability to heal and fight disease. Gratitude also allows us to soften and become humble, noticing the abundance all around us at any given moment. The emphasis is on given. This life can be viewed as a precious gift that has been bestowed on worthy recipients. Yes, that's you—WORTHY. This can take some of the pressure off us to create a "perfect life" and instead encourage us to open to our own divine, always perfect, nature.

There is never a moment when we cannot find something to be grateful for. Try it! Even your very breath is a gift! In this moment of being united with the spirit of humble appreciation we open the gateway to joy and freedom. Our troubles can be washed away, as if by a magic potion, when we see through the eyes of gratitude.

As I gaze into my own heart, like a mirror, it reflects the beauty of my inner and outer life and I am awash in gratitude and filled with joy.

JEWEL THOUGHT

BREATH AWARENESS

Practice Breath Awareness (page 17) and allow yourself to become aware of the gift that is your natural breathing.

Choose a comfortable seated position, such as Easy Pose or Thunderbolt Pose (page 15), or sit in a chair. Soften into the present moment with the breath for a minimum of 1 minute or 10 breaths before adding the mudra.

ATMANJALI MUDRA *(Reverence to the Heart Seal)*

- Bring the hands together in a prayer position in front of your heart but not touching your body.
- The fingers and base of the palms touch each other but keep an open space in the center of the palms—enough to hold a small butterfly safely.
- Lean a few inches forward with the head bowed. This position symbolizes the opening of your heart as you allow it to pour into your hands, which protect the flame of your inner light.
- Hold the position for 10–30 rounds of breath or up to 3 minutes.

prosperity **a rich life**

One dictionary definition of prosperity is: "a successful, flourishing, or thriving condition." That really says it all. We most often equate "prosperity" with the state of our bank account, and while that certainly is a big piece of a prosperous life in a typical interpretation, it doesn't really capture the full essence of the energy of prosperity the way the above definition does. To be prosperous is to experience a thriving condition.

Likewise, the definition of rich is: "plentiful, abundant, generous, bountiful."

These definitions capture the tone and feeling of expansiveness and freedom. Money is a form of energy exchange, having its origins in the barter system. To simplify the exchange in the event that what you had to barter wasn't what the other person needed, or vice versa, the commodity of money was invented to hold value for needed items. Money is the exchange of energy and value. While everyone might agree that feeling rich and prosperous has its foundation in feeling secure financially, that is not a guarantee. In order to experience a true thriving condition and to flourish, we must experience a sense of freedom and expansion with what we already have, and more to the point, who we are.

One way to tap into this liberating view of prosperity is to express gratitude for what you have. Pay attention and notice the bounty that is everywhere in your life from where you are sitting right now. The universe is percolating with abundance and we are channels for the energy of this limitless force.

If you find yourself getting into a state of lack, whatever it may stem from— fear of losing your health, practical money matters, a sense of not enough

Gratitude is the fertile soil ...

time—press pause for a moment and notice what you have. Tune in to the moment and literally look around. Notice everything that is with you in that moment from your body to the room you are in to what you are wearing. Observe that you have breath, eyes to read with, a mind to think, and so on. Feel that you are the source of those things that you seek. You are part of the richness of the universe and not cut off from its prosperous, abundant nature, unless you think it so. Feel your value as part of the world and feel your energy as your greatest investment for your future and the future of the world.

When we tend to our mind, body, and spirit, we can reconnect with bartering in its most perfect form—you have something to give in each moment, no matter how small, and the universe is always ready and willing to give back. In order to fulfill your desires for any type of abundance and prosperity, be clear that it is to the highest good of all concerned, know that your success will surely bring bounty and enrichment to all, and remember you are a powerful generating source for all that you seek.

BELLOWS BREATH

This stimulating breath can build confidence and vitality. Come into a seated position (page 15) and practice one round of the breath (page 23). Then add the mudra, if you like, and continue with the breath as described.

This practice is not recommended during pregnancy or for those with hypertension or panic disorder. Instead, practice *Ujjayi Breath* for 1–3 minutes.

... *from which prosperity grows*

All that I desire comes to me easily and
I accept it with grace and appreciation.

KUBERA MUDRA *(God of Wealth)*

This mudra pulls together the forces of Jupiter (guidance, ambition, joy), Mars (will, action), and Saturn (responsibility, new gateways). After completing your rounds of Bellows Breath, continue to hold the mudra with a focused intention and relax for as long as you like.

- Bring thumb (Mars), index (Jupiter), and middle (Saturn) fingertips together on each hand.
- The ring finger touches the base pad of the thumb and the pinky finger touches the center of the palm.
- Bend your elbows and rest the backs of your hands on your legs.

intuition and wisdom
the guru is you

Intuition is like a muscle that can't be located in the body but when awakened, exercised, and strong is undeniable. The feeling of knowing something without logic, reason, or even information is mystical, yet common. The biggest difficulty with intuition is trusting it. We may have a hunch or gut feeling (often felt in the solar plexus) that is hard to ignore and yet we will reason it away, or discount it for lack of solid evidence. It's also easy to get confused when hopes and fears masquerade as intuition.

One way to look at intuition is as a refined and elevated version of instinct. Instinct is described as a learned behavior that becomes automatic while intuition is a feeling that arises seemingly out of thin air. This is where wisdom comes in and brings them together. We often hear that we carry ancestral patterns, coding, and core beliefs from the beginning of time. In every culture, stories exist of "women's wisdom" that led to health cures, averted disasters, and more. Perhaps when we are not complicating matters with the need for logic, reason, and material proof, we are privy to an ancient instinctual wisdom that is experienced as intuition. Perhaps trusting our intuition can become a learned and very valuable behavior—an instinct.

I often hear, "How do I know if it's my intuition or just my mind?" That's a very good question because the mind is tricky and full of pesky thoughts that camouflage themselves as truth. Ironically, we are very easily persuaded by what comes from the mind, and yet so suspicious of the information coming from the body or energy body. When a rabbit freezes in terror and nothing seems to be near, is that instinct or intuition? It's most likely not a thought, as we know them. Either way the rabbit trusts that feeling in her body and hightails it out of there. Yet we tend to settle for debate. I once ignored my intuition so intensely that I was mugged. My mind wanted proof of what there was to fear and my body said run. I have not made that mistake again! I have also experienced numerous life-altering miracles following intuitive flashes.

So here is the answer to the question. The body doesn't know how to lie. It responds out of a deep knowing, and feels with a kind of sensitivity unknown to the mind. So if you wonder if it's your mind or your intuition talking, get quiet enough to observe the sensations in your body. If you feel peace and ease and relaxation, that's good information. If you feel edgy and fueled with adrenaline, pay close attention. In this way, we can start to separate the chatter from the knowing presence of spirit energy. A guru is someone who brings you from dark to light. When we are in tune with our higher nature and tapping into deeper wisdom, we guide ourselves to the light.

UJJAYI BREATH

Sit, stand, or lie down (page 15) to practice *Ujjayi Breath* (page 18). Imagine your breath is washing away confusion to reveal peace, clarity, and understanding. If adding the mudra, you can do so right away. Focus your attention on the third eye between your eyebrows and do 10–30 rounds of breath. Then relax into stillness.

THE WISDOM THAT LIES BENEATH

When we turn inward for guidance, the first stumbling block is the waves of thoughts that masquerade as wisdom. But under this turbulent surface, there is vast awareness. The oceanic sound of Ujjayi Breath can sweep away the chaos when too many thoughts compete for attention, acting like a golden key for the treasure chest at the ocean's floor, wherein lie the jewels of inner guidance, intuition, and deep wisdom.

NAGA MUDRA *(The Mudra of Deeper Insight)*

This mudra invokes Naga, the snake goddess, known for wisdom, supernatural strength, and shrewdness.

- Place one palm over the other and cross thumbs. It doesn't matter which thumb or hand is on top.
- Raise your hands in front of your chest or set them on your chest, whichever is more comfortable for you.
- If you are seeking clarity regarding a question or problem, bring it into your mind, and then relax and listen.

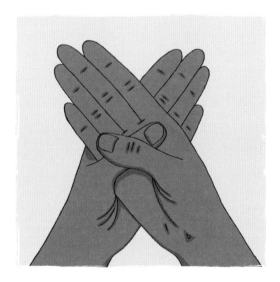

stress reduction and feeling chronically rushed
one breath at a time

Nothing can rob you of your *joi de vivre* as much as being chronically rushed. This insidious source of stress has begun to feel like a cultural epidemic. If you are experiencing this, you may feel that you are "up against the clock" and your life doesn't seem to be your own. One piece of evidence that you are feeling imprisoned by a persistent shortage of time is when your mantra has become "I don't have time!" and "We are running out of time!" and "There's no time!" Your nervous system is now put on high alert and the resulting adrenaline rush may become chronic. The snowball effect is impatient behavior, lack of focus, and absentmindedness, which can unleash feelings of guilt and inadequacy that wreak havoc on self-esteem. This can negatively impact your sense of personal power, which is seated in the same energy center as joy—the solar plexus.

In this scenario, life is a race and only the swiftest will win; but life is not a thing to be won but an experience to be lived. Our connection to time is a relationship that requires awareness and sensitivity in order for our lives to feel both productive and harmonious. We truly have more power than we might

Inhale and feel peace , exhale and release... take life one breath at a time

think we have and it serves us well to put some thought (and time!) into this partnership. A life of chronic rushing overtaxes the immune system, releases an overload of stress hormones, and leads to premature aging among other unsavory side effects.

Here we invoke Hindu goddess Kali for our breath and mudra. Kali, also known as Dirga, is the fierce yet compassionate mother energy, and time is her dominion. She cuts through ego and illusion and helps us to harness our true power through tough compassion. This directs us toward our inner strength to slow down and find center. In this way we serve ourselves, and everyone in our lives, from a grounded and compassionate place. So, to share one of my favorite quotes, "Don't just do something—sit there!"

THREE-PART BREATH

To begin the breath practice, stand with your legs hip-width apart or sit comfortably on the floor or in a chair. On the floor sit in Easy Pose and in a chair make sure both feet are planted on the floor. Take a clearing breath by inhaling through your nose deeply and exhaling through an open mouth completely. Now begin Three-part Breath (page 19).

For extra tension release, you can stick your tongue out toward your chin while you vigorously exhale. Either practice this breath alone for 5–10 rounds minimum or add *Kali Mudra* (see overleaf).

I am strong and calm. I have all the time
I need. I am eternal.

JEWEL THOUGHT

KALI MUDRA

- Interlace your hands except for your index fingers.
- Cross your left thumb over your right thumb.
- Place the hands at the navel center pointing directly forward.
- Relax your shoulders and close your eyes.

Hold the mudra and practice the breath for 5–20 rounds. If you are feeling inspired at any point, you can add the Kali Sword below. This more rigorous version cuts through feelings of powerlessness with a "sword."

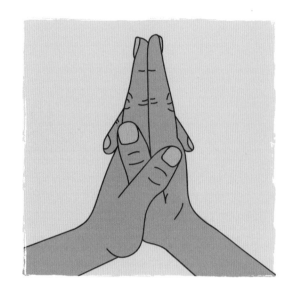

Kali Mudra with Sword

- Take the mudra as instructed above.
- With straight arms point the mudra over your head.
- Keep following the instructions for Three-part Breath (page 19) and on a vigorous exhale bring the arms straight down like a sword to point to the floor.
- This can be done with the tongue extension on the exhale or with the mouth closed.
- Practice 3–6 rounds. Then sit with the mudra at navel center, breathing deeply and slowly from a place of strength and grace. Feel your power and flood yourself with compassion.

anxiety the elephant in every room

Anxiety is a "thing" in both senses of the word. It's a trend (a serious trend) and a condition, and it's taking over. It's not unlike the 1982 movie "The Thing," which tells the story of a group of research scientists seeking to tame and rid their Antarctic camp of the vicious "thing" that is picking them off one by one. The fields of psychiatry, psychology, and mindfulness are trying to keep up with and contain this voracious and prevalent condition.

According to dictionary definitions, the two main categories for anxiety are:

1   A feeling of worry, nervousness, or unease, typically about an imminent event or something with an uncertain outcome.
2   A nervous disorder characterized by a state of excessive uneasiness and apprehension, typically with compulsive behavior or panic attacks.

One is situational and passing, and the other is chronic and perpetual. Among the difficulties that we are facing on a global scale, one is that the world is now full of "imminent events" with "uncertain outcomes" and social media and the internet are reminding us, on a moment to moment basis, of our instability. It's almost impossible to escape interruptions and distractions that deliver a constant parade of possible calamities. Combine this with the genetics that lead to severe disorders, environmental factors, and personal situations and we see that anxiety is, indeed, in most every room. Globally, about 1 in 13 people have anxiety—in the U.S. it's 1 in 8 (Futurity.org/Health and Medicine), and in the UK, more than 1 in 10 people are likely to have an anxiety disorder at some point in their life (Anxiety UK).

Before we get too blue, let's acknowledge the elephant by saying it's normal to have anxiety! It's not pleasant, but it's part of being human.

Certainly, low-grade and situational anxiety are easier to alleviate than the other kind, but even severe cases can be treated with great success. The shortlist of treatments usually features yoga and mindfulness, and along with other appropriate protocols, they bring light to the end of the tunnel.

The magic of mudras and breath in handling anxiety is that we have something very tangible to hook us into the present. Much of the activity in an anxious mind is the way it nervously jumps to future and past, seeking to control possible outcomes, or relive and redo the past. Despite the fact that these are both futile attempts at control, because the future is only projection and the past is, well, over, we try our best to affect them. This is exhausting, defeating, and anxiety provoking. By utilizing the ancient and powerful techniques we have in yoga we strengthen our mind's ability to stay present. As Victor Frankel said: "Everything can be taken from a man but one thing, the last of the human freedoms—to choose one's attitude in any given set of circumstances, to choose one's own way." When choosing the right attitude is elusive, we can practice choosing "Now" and begin from there.

EQUAL BREATH

We will use the square version of this technique because it draws the attention to the present and calms a nervous mind even more than the standard technique (page 18). Sit comfortably (page 15), inhale to the count of 4, hold the breath in for a count of 4, exhale to the count of 4, and hold the breath out for 4. After a practice round, add the mudra if you would like to, and then practice 10 rounds and rest. Continue for longer if desired.

In this moment I choose peace.

JEWEL THOUGHT

VAYU MUDRA (AIR MUDRA)

Too much air in the body is said to create instability and this mudra uses fire energy to suppress the air. It is also effective in reducing tremors for people with Parkinson's Disease.

- Fold your index finger to the base of your thumb on each hand.
- Press your thumb gently but firmly into the first joint of your index finger.
- Extend your middle, ring, and pinky fingers, holding them together.
- Place your hands, facing up or down, on your thighs.

focus make good things happen

Focus pocus! The magic of focus cannot be underrated. In a world filled with shiny things, moving at lightning speed, developing the ability to sustain focus can be the difference between a good idea that sits in a drawer and the launch of an exciting new company that changes the world for the better. It can be the difference between half a blog post and a novel, or a couple of days on a treadmill and running a 10K. Some of us have the knack for it, despite the culture, most parts of which seem to be in a race to disrupt our attention spans. But some of us have always been a little distracted, and might find the current climate exacerbates the tendency to follow every passing fanciful thought.

In order to hold focus without force and strain, we most certainly need a level of interest in what we are focusing on. But even when we are creatively engaged, we may require a little battery charge at the intersection between interest and action. A Sanskrit term, *tapas* (not the Spanish appetizer!), is apt. This refers to the quality of inner fire, or *agni*, that must be ignited and sustained for long enough to burn off the impurities in the body or mind. When yoga *asanas* (poses) are practiced in a way that brings heat to the body, the toxins and impurities (or we could say that which distracts the system from purification) are removed. Inherent in the concept of *tapas* is the quality of discipline, of which focus is an essential ingredient. When we practice developing focus, we are holding our attention on something, which creates an inner fire and chases away the obstacles that invariably land in our way. A key component in cultivating this inner fire is a clear and engaging goal. Yes, yoga is goal oriented! The goal may be to sit still and be present and to accept what is, but that is still a goal. As long as we are in the moment on the way to achieving the goal, and do not cause ourselves undue suffering if we fail to reach our destination, we are in the practice.

Whether you are engaging your focus to recall something you forgot, to listen wholeheartedly to a friend, or to bring your grandest vision to life, you can light the fire, build some stamina, and relax into focus. When we do this, good things tend to happen.

BREATH AWARENESS

Using the physical sensation of breathing as an anchor for your mind is a great way to increase your ability to focus. If you have trouble, remember that all the wonderful things you wish to achieve and experience require you to hold your attention upon them. Breath Awareness is described on page 17. Add the mudra if you like, and practice for a minimum of 3 minutes or count 30 breaths.

HAKINI MUDRA *(Power or Rule Mudra)*

This mudra generates power to rule over a restless mind.

- Bring the fingertips of the right hand to touch the fingertips of the left hand.
- Your elbows are bent and your hands are in front of your ribcage or where it feels natural.
- Use a slight pressure coming from your arms to press the fingertips together.
- Use a sand timer, clock, or inner clock to hold the mudra while focusing on the breath for 3 minutes minimum.

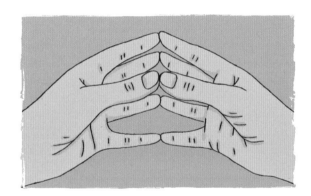

I am steady and awake. My mind is strong and clear.

JEWEL THOUGHT

grief **hold your own hand**

Few emotions can run us through the wringer like grief can. Most commonly associated with loss, it hits in the heart with a powerful thud and a lasting ache. As one friend described it, "It's like a boot on my chest 24 hours a day." According to the powerful and insightful work of Elisabeth Kübler-Ross and David Kessler, grief has five stages: denial, anger, bargaining, depression, acceptance. As Kessler points out in his writings, these divisions are not meant to tidy up what is inherently messy in the world of very real human emotions, but to shed light on what many experience as they travel a road of mourning.

Yoga allows us to experience our feelings while giving space for the body to let go of them when the time is right. Our intelligent bodies are very adept at storing things for us, and even taking on pain when it's too much for the conscious mind to bear. This gives the brain a certain relief, and offers us the opportunity to tuck away a feeling that won't let go and causes us suffering.

However, for optimal physical and mental health, fluidity with feelings is important. It's necessary to allow space and time for our feelings to be felt and heard. It's also essential that we are mindful in letting them go. Grief can be a dance with intricate steps. We hold our own hand, honor our feelings with unconditional love, understanding, and acceptance, and try to stay flexible and present. When grieving, we need more kindness and patience with ourselves than ever before. Spend the love and energy that is seeking what's missing from your life on yourself. Love is energy and cannot be destroyed but seeks to be realized. It is like the light that always finds its way

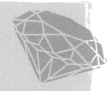

I let go of the sadness in my body.
I let go in love.

JEWEL THOUGHT

into a room. As the great Sufi poet Rumi said, "The wound is the place where the light enters you." Heartbreak, loss, sadness, and despair might threaten to tear us apart, but they can bring us together with the sweetness of compassion.

The practice described here is different in origin from the others in the book. It is a mudra practice from Chinese Medicine rather than from the yoga of India, and it is always combined with the breathing practice. It's wonderful for grief, depression, sadness, and anxiety. It is also said to bring good fortune and enhance personal magnetism.

TSE MUDRA WITH BREATH RETENTION AND OM

- Sit comfortably, elbows bent and forearms extended to the side, or place your hands on your legs. See which feels the most calming and comfortable for you.
- Place the thumb tip of each hand at the base of each pinky finger.
- Fold your remaining fingers over the thumb as you slowly inhale.
- Hold your breath and silently make the sound of Om in your head, feeling the vibration and "hearing" the sound in your right ear.
- Slowly exhale as you draw your navel to your spine.
- Open your hands and imagine all your pain, fear, and sadness leaving your body.

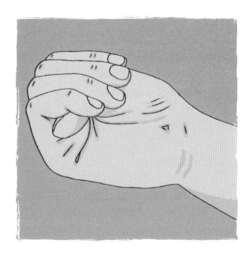

- Do this a minimum of 7 times and a maximum of 49 times, according to the Taoist monks.
- When you have finished, rest your arms on your legs if they were lifted, and quietly focus on the jewel thought if you like.

vitality lit from within

When I first began my yoga path, my future husband brought me to a class taught by a 75-year-old man, Frank, who found yoga at the age of 65. When he first stepped onto a mat, he was in terrible health due to an alcohol problem and a four-pack a day cigarette habit. He was overweight, had lung issues, rheumatoid arthritis, and a leaky heart valve, and he said yoga saved him from the cemetery. By the time I took his class, which was the most challenging class I had ever taken, he was a spitfire. His bright eyes twinkled and gleamed with mischief and wisdom. He would take brief pauses from his cues and inspirational words to grab his big toe and throw his leg up in the air like a teenage cheerleader. He was fit, exuberant, dynamic, joyful, powerful, and vital. Fortunately, we became close friends and I learned a lot about vitality from him, until his passing at the age of 85. He was still teaching yoga.

When I'm energized, I feel I can take on the world. There is nothing I can't do. I feel unstoppable, like lightning. When my energy is flat, the idea of making dinner seems like a pipe dream, let alone being an inspired teacher, a present and engaged parent and spouse, a caring friend, and so on. Our physical energy level truly affects our mood, vision, logic, and attitude. It has been a journey to discover the right recipe for a consistent and natural flow of vital life force. Of course, I have days when I'm tired due to any number of variables, but more often than not I feel zesty and effervescent. I credit this to some good genes, a healthy diet, a loving and supportive family, and passion for my work. But the thread that really pulls it together is my practice. I didn't come to it hanging by a thread like Frank, but I embrace it like a lifeline now.

Vitality is more than just physical energy; it's access to the vastness of cosmic consciousness and source energy that ignites the life force, or *prana*. If we can get *prana* to circulate freely through the whole system, we can increase vitality. To be able to maintain vitality, the body must be primed to hold the light in a way that illuminates it, and all who are in its presence. This is possible and available for everyone, and a perfect way to step into the light, at any moment, is breath and mudra.

SKULL SHINING BREATH OR SUN BREATH

Choose which one of these two breaths suits you at the moment (pages 23 and 20). Skull Shining Breath is not recommended during pregnancy or for those with hypertension or panic disorder. Otherwise they are both excellent for circulation and pranic flow. Once seated (page 15) practice one round, then add the mudra if you wish, using both hands with Skull Shining Breath and the left hand with Sun Breath—the right hand is used for the breath. If you are left handed, reverse the hands. Practice 3 rounds minimum of Skull Shining Breath and 10 rounds minimum of Sun Breath.

PRAN MUDRA *(Life-force Mudra)*

This mudra will stimulate the even flow of blood and *prana* in the body.

- Bring your thumbs, ring and pinky fingers together on each hand.
- Index and middle fingers are together and extended.
- Place your hands, palms up, on your thighs.

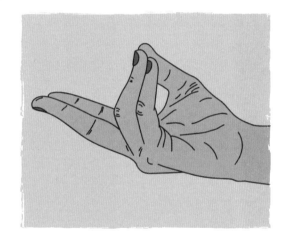

I am lit up with the creative life force
of the universe.

JEWEL THOUGHT

kindness and compassion
what the world needs now

It has been said that humanity will not have true lasting peace until we can hold compassion for all living things. This might, at certain moments, seem daunting or impossible, but the larger challenge and the golden key to peace may actually be self-compassion first. While it is true that we can do a lot of good in the world and still carry a certain amount of angst and self-loathing around on the journey, we are not as effective as representatives of compassion without first-hand embodied compassion.

Some are concerned that if they practice too much kindness on themselves, they may become lazy or "too soft" and not maintain important disciplines. This is not to be feared if you are practicing true compassion, which is simply empathy and understanding. Whatever your circumstances may be, you can keep to your highest standards while showing yourself true compassion.

Thich Nhat Hanh (world peace leader, living guru, and author) teaches that what we really need is to be heard and to experience some understanding. Practicing this on yourself can loosen the grip of perfectionism and open the door to a deep empathy that begins at home and reaches far

One act of kindness can bring lasting joy to many

> My heart expands to extend kindness
> and compassion to myself and everyone.
>
> **JEWEL THOUGHT**

and wide. This requires that we honor both the dark and the light that exists in us all. When we can stretch ourselves enough to embrace our beautiful bits, including our warts and scars, the kind path appears. Our judgments toward ourselves and others soften, our awareness of our connectedness emerges, and we become more productive in bringing about peace as we see our sameness through shared human experience. We all struggle, have fears and disappointments, and suffer from confusion, and we all seek joy, peace, light, and love. If you are the homeless woman on the street or the executive on the top floor, you are made of the same stuff. Animals on land and sea and humans are sharing this planet and the entire cosmos and it's in our best interest to try to understand and support one another. When we truly recognize our core equality, despite circumstances and appearances, we can hold each other's sorrows and dreams as a collective vision and unite our energy toward the highest good for all.

Begin by looking at yourself in the mirror. Look beyond what you do and don't like. See the soul looking at you and remember that you are divine light and love and you are doing the best you can with what you have in this moment. Then look upon everyone today with gentle eyes. The world needs more kindness, not less. Now let's relax and breathe and mudra together.

THREE-PART BREATH

Sit comfortably (page 15) and begin the breath (page 19). As you inhale, imagine that you are bringing light and peace into your heart center, and as you exhale release anger, fear, and hard feelings toward yourself and others. Do one round and then bring in the mudra if you wish. With or without the mudra, take 10–30 rounds of breath.

VARADA MUDRA (THE GESTURE OF GENEROSITY)

This mudra signifies compassion, mercy, and devotion to the salvation of humankind. The left hand is in *Varada* and the right hand can take one of any number of mudras along with it. Here we relax the hand, palm up, in the lap in a gesture of openness.

- Place your left hand, palm up, on your left knee.
- Keep the fingers relaxed and tilting toward the floor.
- Bring your right hand into your lap palm up.

love and healthy relationships
start with you

"Vulnerageous" is a wonderful word created by a loving couple who have attended my classes for years. Courageous vulnerability. That's how I think of true love.

Another powerful word is *aparigraha*, Sanskrit for non-attachment or non-grasping. When it comes to love, it seems counterintuitive to imagine loving without attachment but the expression of pure love is an act that frees the giver and receiver. We tend to confuse love with something to be earned or bestowed, as though we own it to begin with. Love is the creative life force in the universe. We can't own it any more than a fish owns the ocean. As it flows through us we may inhabit moments of surrender and acceptance. If we nurture and allow this opening to deep self-love, we have the potential for truly nourishing healthy relationships. If we bypass this crucial opportunity to allow a sense of deep connection, we may try to own the love of others, to restore this broken current. This can lead to clinging, grasping, fear, and loss. It can happen with lovers, family, children, friends, or anyone. Unhealthy attachments develop into the ego's idea of who our loved ones should or shouldn't be, or how they should behave in order to continue to receive our love. Although we thrive in the light of loving relationships, the foundation upon which all our bonds depend is the relationship to self.

In me I see you, in you I see me,
We flow with each other in sweet harmony

When we practice courageous vulnerability, forgiveness, kindness, and loving ourselves, we can move past the ego's opinions, and find joy as we surf and swim in an ocean of love. It's what we came from, what we dwell in, and what we seek. It's the force that beats your heart, breathes your lungs, lifts the moon, and sets the sun. When we are pinched off from our shared source of divine love by not accepting ourselves as the very ocean we seek safe harbor within, we can't extend true love to those we wish to touch the most. It's taken me decades to truly understand that while we might be able to love someone without self-love, it will not be the kind of love we deserve or are capable of. As we define a new layer of appreciation and empathy for ourselves, we deepen and strengthen our bonds with our loved ones—and there is a big difference between bonds and shackles.

UJJAYI BREATH

Come into a comfortable seated or standing position and follow the instructions for *Ujjayi Breath* on page 18.

Take a few rounds of breath and then add the mudra opposite. If you prefer to skip the mudra, you can lie down and breathe, imagining you are floating in a sea of love.

I am love. I gain my strength from giving and receiving love freely.

JEWEL THOUGHT

GANESHA MUDRA *(The Remover of Obstacles Mudra)*

This mudra gives us courage and strengthens the heart center. It helps to dissolve obstacles or recognize them as opportunities to grow and deepen our connection to self.

- Place the back of your left hand at the level of your heart, horizontally, a few inches from your chest.
- Place the palm side of your right hand in front of your left hand and hook the fingers of your right hand into the fingers of the left.
- Your elbows are out to the sides and level with your hands.
- As you inhale, pull against the fingers creating tension in the arms, chest, and fingers.
- Exhale and relax your arms but keep the mudra.
- Do 5 rounds and rest. Continue for as long as desired, adding the jewel thought when ready.

happiness soul sweets

Nothing says happy like a smile. A smile is only a moment away from a laugh and a laugh is like a tickle in the heart. Happy is a special fizzy feeling that is light, bubbly, and carefree. It's flying into the sky on a swing with a popsicle in your hand. It's the first swim of the summer or a warm mug of chocolate after the cold satisfaction of a well-packed snowman. It's being so close with someone you can make each other laugh without trying.

The beauty of happiness is that it's mixed up in the laboratory of our bodies with wizard-like precision when we place ourselves in particular situations, such as being with people who accept and value us. Affection, connection, fun time, creativity, adventure, curiosity, and feeling comfortable with ourselves are all part of placing ourselves in an environment, or state of being, that can produce happiness. We are wired to seek what makes us feel good, again and again. It's a perfect formula, especially when we factor in that the release of the happy hormones (serotonin, oxytocin, dopamine, and endorphins) is excellent for our health. The immune system gets a boost, the circulatory system flows nicely, the release of stress hormones decreases, and even the aging process can be slowed. And on that note, we are all going to get wrinkles so they might as well be the jolly kind!

One of my favorite ways of keeping happiness within arm's reach is to make a list and practice appreciation for the things on the list at least once a week. Just read the list and say thank you after each thing. Watch the list grow as you add new people and experiences into your life. One of my "go to" happy things is good books. Another is crazy time and laughter with my daughter. The list doesn't have to be fancy or complicated. Whatever says happy to you, take time for it daily. That regular dose of cheer is like a vitamin, full of benefits and able to fill in the gaps when you need extra support. In those life moments when sadness has hijacked happiness, after allowing the sadness to be heard, pull out your list and read it. Even if you can't quite get the feeling, you will know that sure as the sun will rise, your spirits will eventually, too. Happiness is cake for the soul and a sweet life is something we all deserve. This breath and mudra practice is sure to bring a smile.

HISSING BREATH

Come into your most comfortable position for this soothing breath (page 24). The shape of the mouth in this breath is a smile and that gets the happy juices flowing! If you wish to add the mudra, do so from the start and then practice the breath and mudra for between 10 and 30 rounds.

HANSI MUDRA *(Swan Mudra)*

This mudra moves the energy upward toward the heart and face to uplift the spirit.

- Bring your thumbs, index, middle and ring fingers together on each hand, pinky fingers extended.
- Either set the back of your hands on your thighs or hold both arms to the side at shoulder height, elbows bent, hands pointing upward.

I am uplifted, happiness flows to me and through me as I glide through my life.

JEWEL THOUGHT

hope is alive

Hope can be a slippery slope. To have hope is essential to moving forward in life. To lose hope is to flounder in despair. To give hope is to hand a candle to someone lost in the dark. It's the gift of light. Some years ago, I received a call from Evelyn, aged 93, who wanted to begin yoga. She was suffering from macular degeneration and it was very frightening for her. This is when the eyes begin to lose sight in a particularly chaotic way. It's like looking through a dim kaleidoscope. The world becomes fragmented, shattered and broken. She had never done anything remotely like yoga in her life and was nervous, desperate, and excited. Upon meeting her I fell in love with her bouffant, her style, her spunk, and her determination. We mostly practiced mudras, simple arm movements and breath, and she began to glow. She couldn't believe she had lived so long on her "regular old breath."

It was during my time with Evelyn that I fell deeply in love with mudras. I saw that a 93-year-old woman who was caged in semi darkness and confusion could be elevated to joy through her hands and breath. Although we spoke often of death and her fears, she began to experience hope about everything. She marveled at the nature of the universe, her ability to laugh, and the mudras that she adored. One day after a year or so of practicing with her, I arrived at her apartment to learn that she was in a coma in hospital. A new sleep medication had affected her badly. I rushed along to find her family gathered in a corner, clearly agitated. As I approached Evelyn they informed me that she wouldn't know I was there. It had been a few days and she hadn't moved, spoken, or fluttered an eyelid. She seemed far away and

I am open, pure, and filled with love.

JEWEL THOUGHT

her breathing was shallow. I held her hand, and told her that I loved her. I said we needed her to get home and back to yoga. After a few minutes, I let go of her hand and prepared to leave. At that moment her hands began to move slowly and she brought her thumbs to her index fingers into the first mudra I'd taught her, *Gyana Mudra*. In this mudra the thumb is symbolic of the divine, and the index finger is the individual. She held it and continued to sleep.

Evelyn recovered and we started up our twice-a-week practice again for another beautiful year. When Evelyn passed away, she left me with a priceless gift. Hope. She showed me that the soul has wings and will always choose to fly when given the chance. She also gifted me the very real understanding of the power of breath and mudras as a language for the heart and soul.

UJJAYI BREATH

Ths breath (page 18) can triumph over fear and invite love. Add the mudra, if you choose to, right away. Take 10–30 rounds of breath.

PADMASANA MUDRA *(Lotus Mudra)*

This mudra is a symbol of purity and connected to the heart chakra. The lotus symbolizes our journey from dark to light as the lotus travels from the murky river bed to the light of day and floats on the surface of the water, clean, pure, and unsoiled despite the journey.

- Place the hands in front of the heart center with the heels of the hands touching.
- Bring the tips of the pinky fingers and thumbs to touch.
- Fan the other fingers open like a fully bloomed lotus flower.

resources

CHRISTINE'S GOLDEN MILK RECIPE

You can buy golden milk, but it's easier and cheaper to make a batch at home that will last a few days. It's the perfect yogi drink with health benefits galore—in particular it's great for joints and reducing inflammation. Have a cup at bedtime and sleep like a baby—only all night long!

4-8 whole cloves

1 small cinnamon stick

3–6 green cardamom pods

½ cup (120ml) of water

1 cup (240ml) milk of your choice, such as cow's milk, almond, soy, coconut or hemp

½ teaspoon ground turmeric

¼ teaspoon freshly ground black pepper

½–1 teaspoon pure extra virgin coconut oil or almond oil (omit this if using coconut milk)

1 teaspoon raw honey or stevia to taste

makes 1 serving

Put the water in a small saucepan and add the cloves, cinnamon stick, and cardamom pods. Bring to a boil for 3–5 minutes.

Add the milk, ground turmeric, pepper, and oil to the saucepan and simmer on low for about 7 minutes, stirring occasionally with a whisk, but do not let it boil. Strain and serve. Add the raw honey or stevia if desired. Let cool before drinking.

To make a batch of golden milk, simply double or triple the quantities as required. The golden milk will keep for 3–5 days, stored in an airtight container in the refrigerator. Reheat in a saucepan on the stove or in the microwave (it is better reheated in a saucepan to retain the healthful properties).

Note: If you cannot obtain whole spices, you can substitute ground spices: ¼ teaspoon of ground cloves, ¼ teaspoon ground cinnamon, and ⅛ teaspoon ground cardamom. In this case, there is no need to boil the spices in water first—simply add the ground spices to the milk, turmeric, pepper, and oil.

BOOKS AND WEBSITES

Asana Pranayama Mudra Bandha by Swami Satyananda Saraswati (Bihar School of Yoga, 2003)

Mudras: Yoga in Your Hands by Gertrud Hirschi (Red Wheel/Weiser, 2016)

Inspiration also comes from the work and teachings of Sabrina Mesko (www.sabrinamesko.com) and Abraham Hicks (www.abraham-hicks.com).

ARTICLES

"How to Keep Computer Screens from Destroying Your Eyes" by Lindsay Abrams, September 2012 (www.theatlantic.com/health/archive/2012/09/how-to-keep-computer-screens-from-destroying-your-eyes/263005)

"How Happiness Boosts the Immune System" by Jo Marchant, November 2013 (www.scientificamerican.com/article/how-happiness-boosts-the-immune-system)

"How Gratitude Changes You and Your Brain" by Joel Wong and Joshua Brown, June 2017 (greatergood.berkeley.edu/article/item/how_gratitude_changes_you_and_your_brain)

"What is Hridaya, the Spiritual Heart?" (hridaya-yoga.com/hridaya-yoga-articles/what-is-hridaya-the-spiritual-heart)

index